HANDS-ON ABCs

ABC Games

by Marilynn G. Barr

LAB20143P
Hands-on ABCs
ABC GAMES
by Marilynn G. Barr

Published by: Little Acorn Books™
Originally published by: Monday Morning Books, Inc.

Entire contents copyright © 2014 Little Acorn Books™

Little Acorn Books
PO Box 8787
Greensboro, NC 27419-0787

Promoting Early Skills for a Lifetime™

Little Acorn Books™
is an imprint of Little Acorn Associates, Inc.

http://www.littleacornbooks.com

Permission is hereby granted to reproduce student materials in this book for non-commercial individual or classroom use. *School-wide or system-wide use is expressly prohibited.

ISBN 978-1-937257-59-0

Printed in the United States of America

Contents

Introduction 4
Letters A-D
   Alphabet Trail Game Board 6
   Spinner and Pawns 8
   Game Board Playing Cards 9
   Alphabet Bingo 10
   Alphabet Die 12
   Color-By-Letter 13
Letters E-I
   Alphabet Trail Game Board 16
   Spinner and Pawns 18
   Game Board Playing Cards 19
   Alphabet Bingo 20
   Alphabet Die 22
   Color-By-Letter 23
Letters J-M
   Alphabet Trail Game Board 27
   Spinner and Pawns 29
   Game Board Playing Cards 30
   Alphabet Bingo 31
   Alphabet Die 33
   Color-By-Letter 34
Letters N-R
   Alphabet Trail Game Board 37
   Spinner and Pawns 39
   Game Board Playing Cards 40
   Alphabet Bingo 41
   Alphabet Die 43
   Color-By-Letter 44

Letters S-V
   Alphabet Trail Game Board 47
   Spinner and Pawns 49
   Game Board Playing Cards 50
   Alphabet Bingo 51
   Alphabet Die 53
   Color-By-Letter 54
Letters W-Z
   Alphabet Trail Game Board 57
   Spinner and Pawns 59
   Game Board Playing Cards 60
   Alphabet Bingo 61
   Alphabet Die 63
   Color-By-Letter 64

Introduction

ABC Games is one of four Hands-on ABC books (**ABC Scissor Skills, ABC Mini Books,** and **ABC Art**) designed to provide alphabet skills practice activities for early learners. Children develop social and fair play skills as they practice recognizing letters and letter sounds and associating letters with alphabet pictures. **ABC Games** also offers matching, following directions, coloring, cutting, gluing, and memory skills practice.

ABC Games features Alphabet Trail Game Boards, spinners, flat pawns, alphabet dice, freestanding pawns, Alphabet Bingo picture and letter cards, and Color-By-Letter cards. Make games in advance for use in the classroom or reproduce and provide a complete set of game patterns (matching game board and spinner, cards, or die, matching letter and alphabet picture Bingo Cards, or Color-By-Letter cards) for each child to take home, color, cut out, assemble, and play with family and friends.

Alphabet Trail Game Boards

Reproduce, color, and cut out each game board half. Trim each center seam and glue each half, matching the center seams, onto a sheet of oak tag, then laminate. Measure, cut, and tape a construction paper pocket to the back of the game board to store matching spinners, pawns, and cards. To play, children each choose a pawn. Each player, in turn, will roll a die, spin, or draw a card. The player then moves his or her pawn to the next space that matches the letter or alphabet picture on the spinner dial, die, or card. Identify and explain consequence and bonus spaces and cards to non-readers and younger children. Play continues until each player reaches THE END.

Spinners and Pawns

Spinner: Reproduce, color, and cut out the spinner. Punch a hole in the center of the spinner and arrow and attach with a brass fastener. Each player, in turn, will spin the arrow. Store the spinner in the construction paper pocket attached to the back of the matching game board.

Pawns: Each Spinner and Pawn page features two sets of pawns. Choose and reproduce one set to accompany each matching trail game board. Color, laminate, then cut out the pawns. Store pawns in the construction paper pocket attached to the back of the matching game board.

Alphabet Cards

Reproduce, color, laminate, and cut apart a set of cards that matches your chosen game board. Shuffle and place the deck of cards face down on the playing surface. Each child, in turn, draws and turns over one card. The player then moves his or her pawn to the next space that matches the alphabet picture or letter on the card. When cards are all used, reshuffle the cards to continue play. Store cards in the construction paper pocket attached to the back of the matching game board.

Dice and Pawns

Die: Reproduce, color, and cut out an oak tag die pattern that matches your chosen game board. Fold the pattern where indicated. Apply glue and secure each tab as you assemble the die. Each player, in turn, rolls the die. The player then moves his or her pawn to the next space that matches the alphabet picture or letter on the die.

Pawns: Reproduce, color, and cut out the pawn patterns. Fold each pawn pattern where indicated and secure with glue, tape, or a staple.

Alphabet Concentration

Reproduce, color, laminate, and cut a set of cards apart. Shuffle and place the cards face down on a playing surface. Each child, in turn, turns over two cards. If the cards match, the player keeps the cards and play continues. If there is no match, the player turns the cards over (in the same positions) and play continues. Play continues until all the cards are matched.

Alphabet Picture Cards

Letter Cards

Reward and Consequence Cards

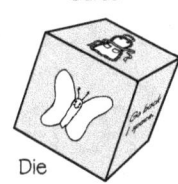
Die

Free-standing Pawn

Alternate Pawns
Color each a different color.

Alphabet Bingo

Alphabet Picture Card Bingo: Reproduce and cut out (do not cut apart) an oak tag alphabet picture card for each child to color. Provide each child with nine flat pawns to use as Bingo tokens. Reproduce and cut apart matching letter cards. Shuffle and place the letter cards face down on a flat surface. Draw a card from the deck. Call out the letter and show the children the card. Have children place a pawn on a picture that starts with the letter on the card. Place the called cards face up on the playing surface. Continue drawing cards and calling out the letters. When a player has placed a pawn on three adjoining spaces (vertically, horizontally, or diagonally), he or she can call out B-I-N-G-O. Check the player's card with your discards. If the player is correct, he or she has won and his or her game ends. If the player is incorrect, he or she continues to play. Continue to play until all players have had a chance to call out B-I-N-G-O.

Letter Card Bingo: Reproduce and cut out (do not cut apart) a colored construction paper letter card for each child. Provide each child with nine flat pawns to use as Bingo tokens. Reproduce and cut apart matching alphabet picture cards. Shuffle and place the picture cards, face down on a flat surface. Draw a card from the deck. Call out the name of the picture and show the children the card. Have children place a pawn on a letter that begins the picture on the card. Place the called cards face up on the playing surface. Continue drawing cards and calling out the picture names. When a player has placed a pawn on three adjoining spaces (vertically, horizontally, or diagonally), he or she can call out B-I-N-G-O. Check the player's card with your discards. If the player is correct, he or she has won and his or her game ends. If the player is incorrect, he or she continues to play. Continue to play until all players have had a chance to call out B-I-N-G-O.

Color-By-Letter Cards

Reproduce, color, laminate, and cut apart a set of the Color-By-Letter cards. Mount each card on a sheet of oak tag slightly larger than the card. Prepare an alphabet practice table with a box filled with Color-By-Letter cards, wipe-off crayons or markers, and paper towel squares. Help each child read the coloring instructions, then have him or her color the card by letter. Create alternate cards with different coloring instructions.

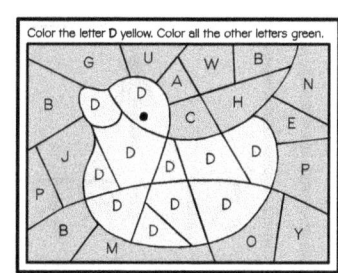

Alphabet Trail Game Board
Letters A-D

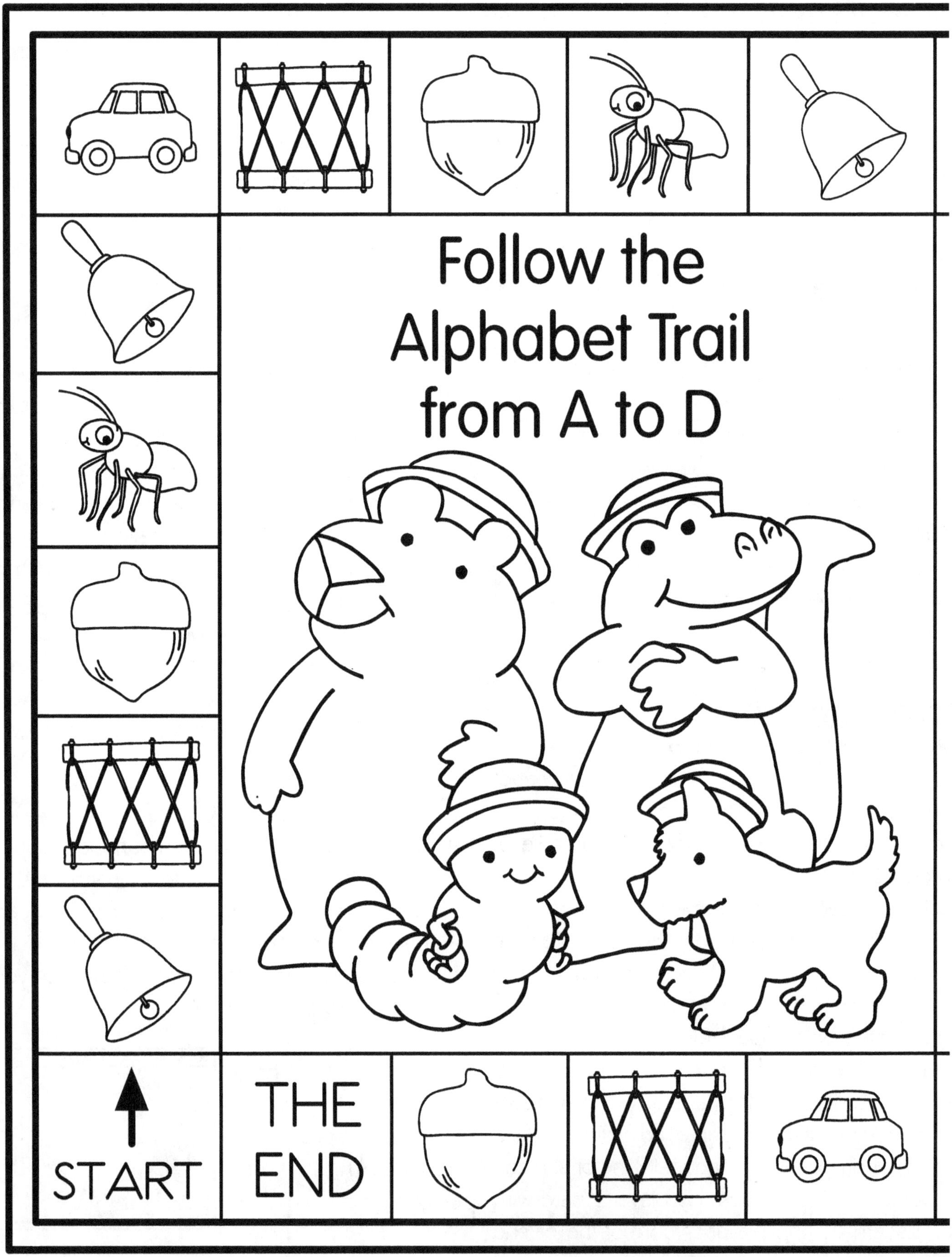

Follow the Alphabet Trail from A to D

START ↑

THE END

Alphabet Trail Game Board
Letters A-D

Place card deck, die, or spinner here.

Spinner and Pawns
Letters A-D

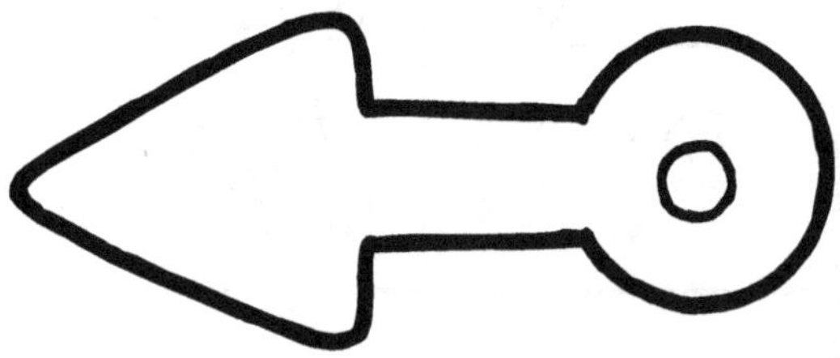

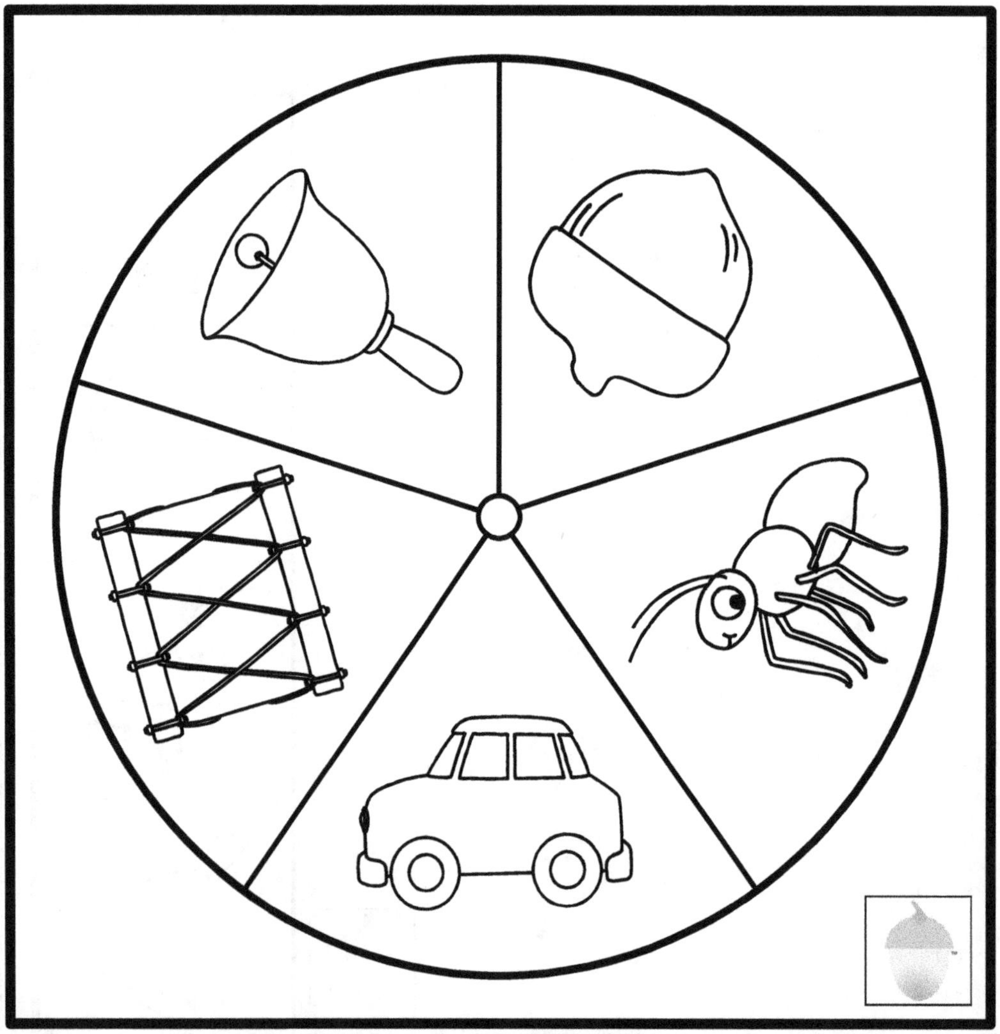

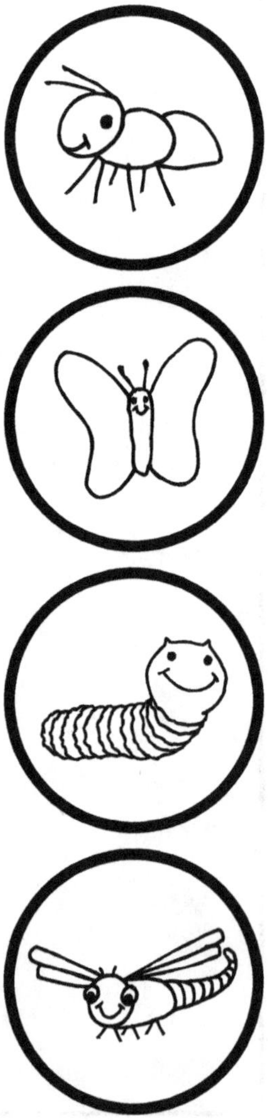

Color each pawn a different color.

Game Board Playing Cards
Letters A-D

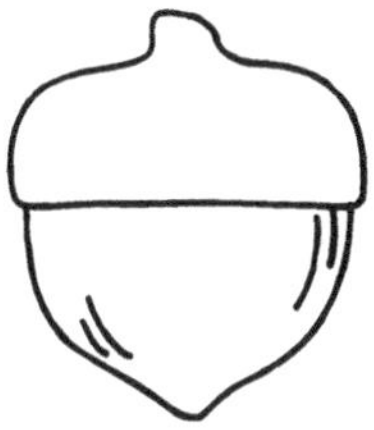

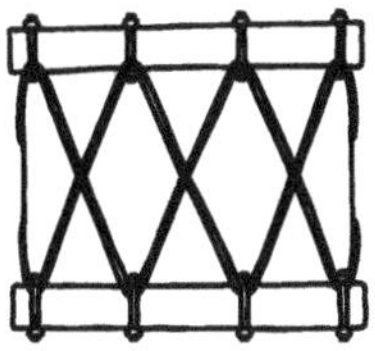

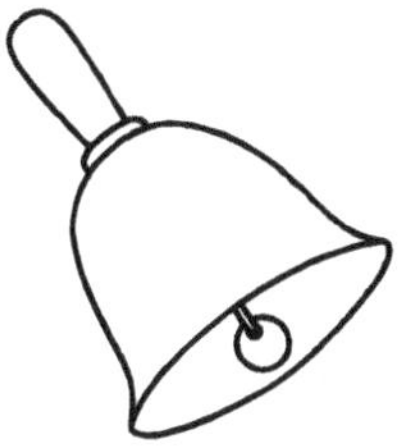

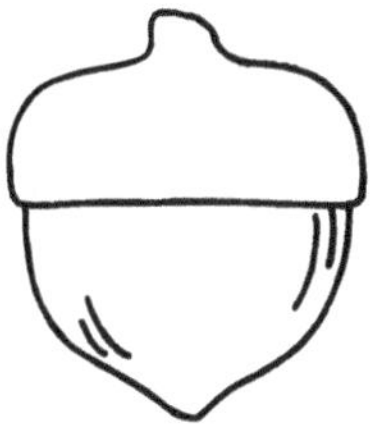

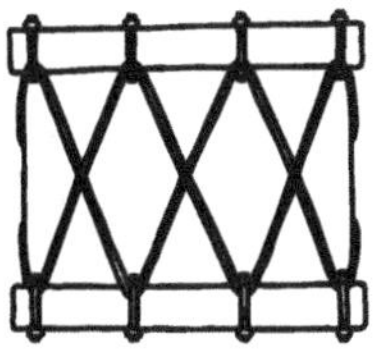

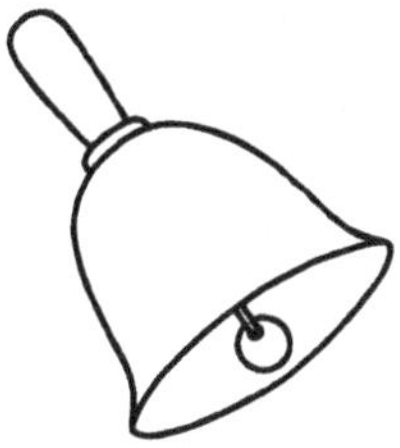

| a | b | c | d | Move forward 1 space. |
| A | B | C | D | Move back 1 space. |

Alphabet Bingo
Alphabet Pictures A-D

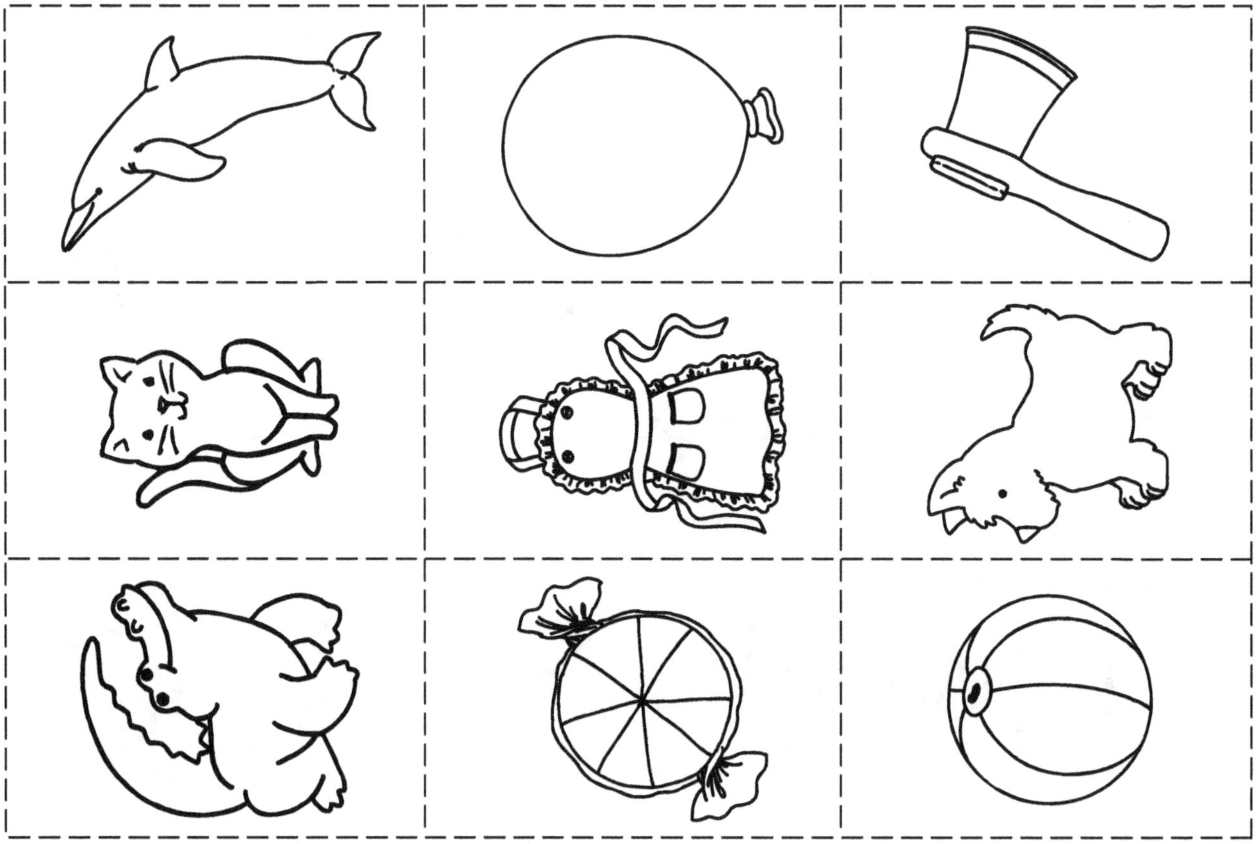

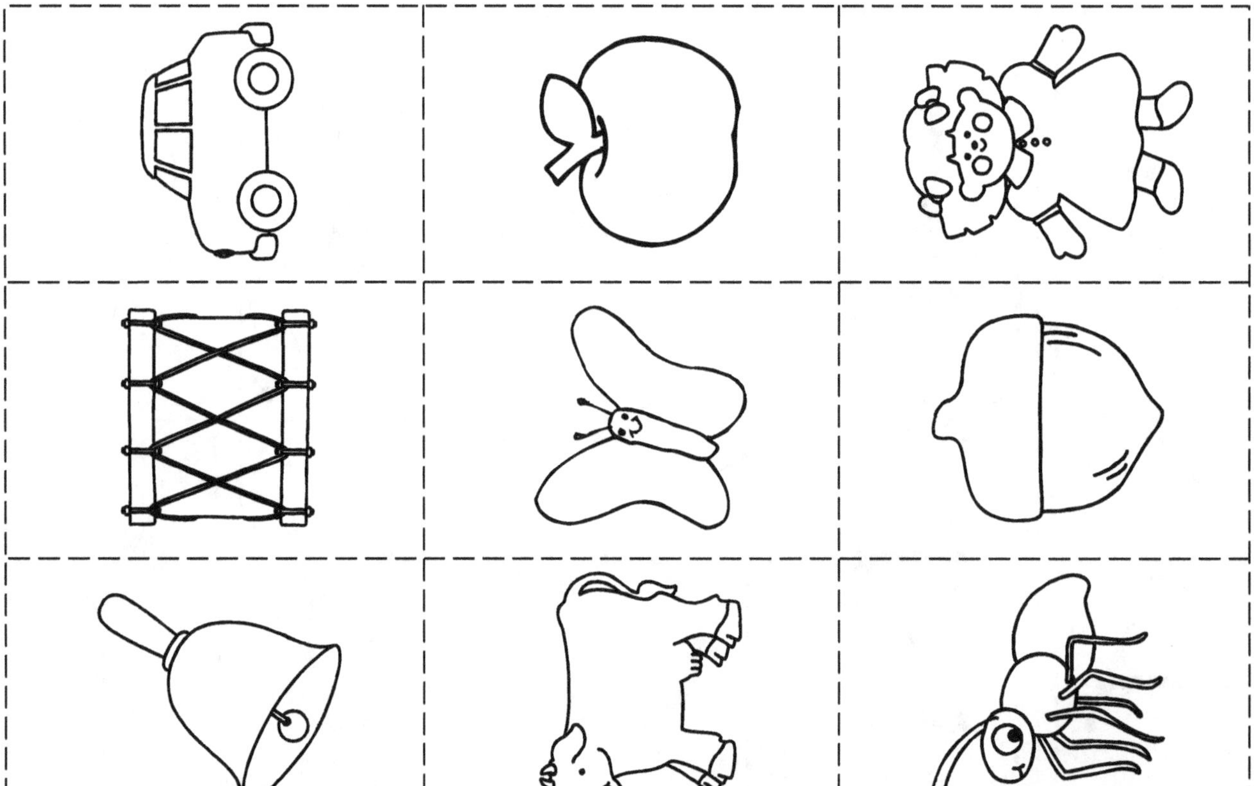

Alphabet Bingo
Letters A-D

d	b	a
c	a	d
a	c	b
D	A	A
B	C	A

Alphabet Die
Letters A-D

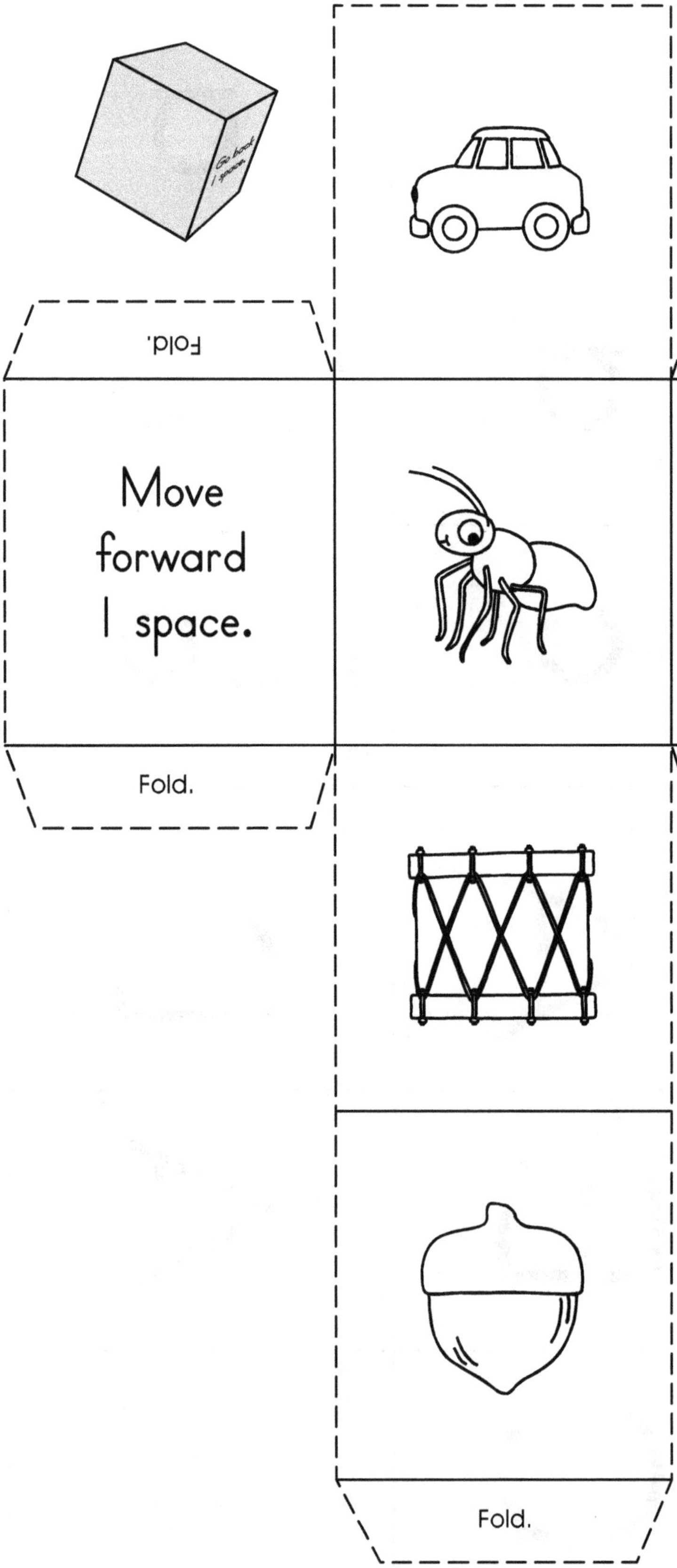

Move forward 1 space.

Fold.

Fold.

Fold.

Fold.

Glue or staple tops together.

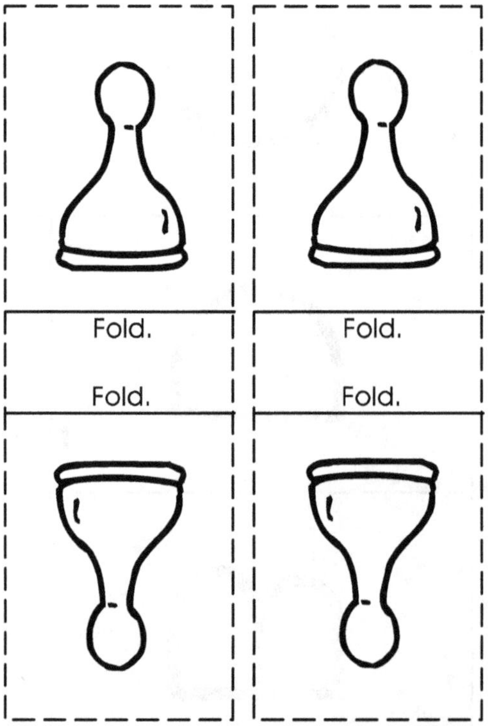

Fold.

Fold. Fold.

Fold. Fold.

Color each pawn a different color.

12 LAB20143P • ABC GAMES • 978-1-937257-59-0 • © 2014 Little Acorn Books™

Color-By-Letter
Letters A and B

Color the **A** shapes red. Color all the other shapes green.

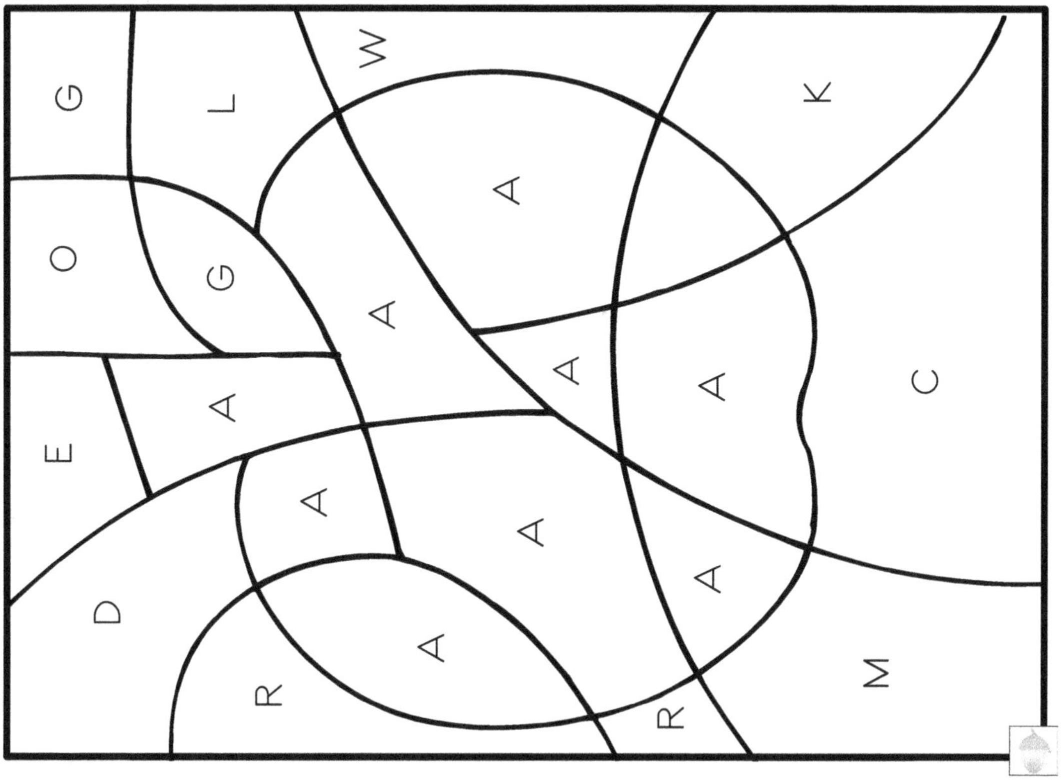

Color the **B** shapes yellow. Color all the other shapes blue.

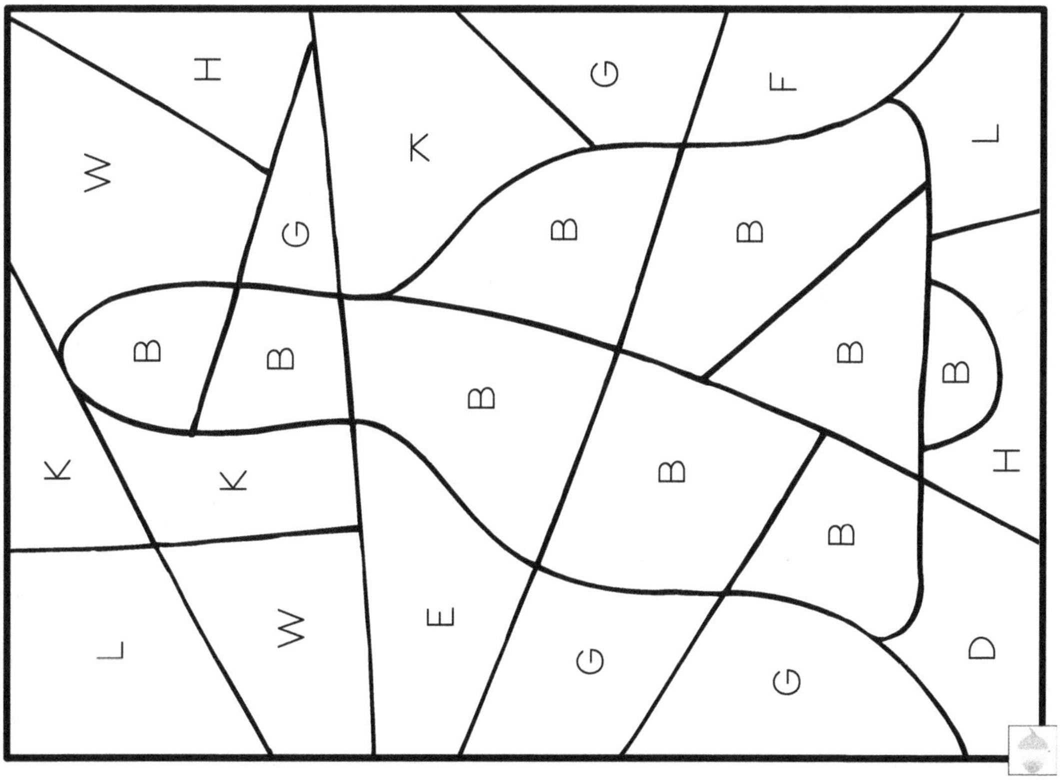

Color-By-Letter
Letters C and D

Color the **C** shapes orange. Color all the other shapes blue.

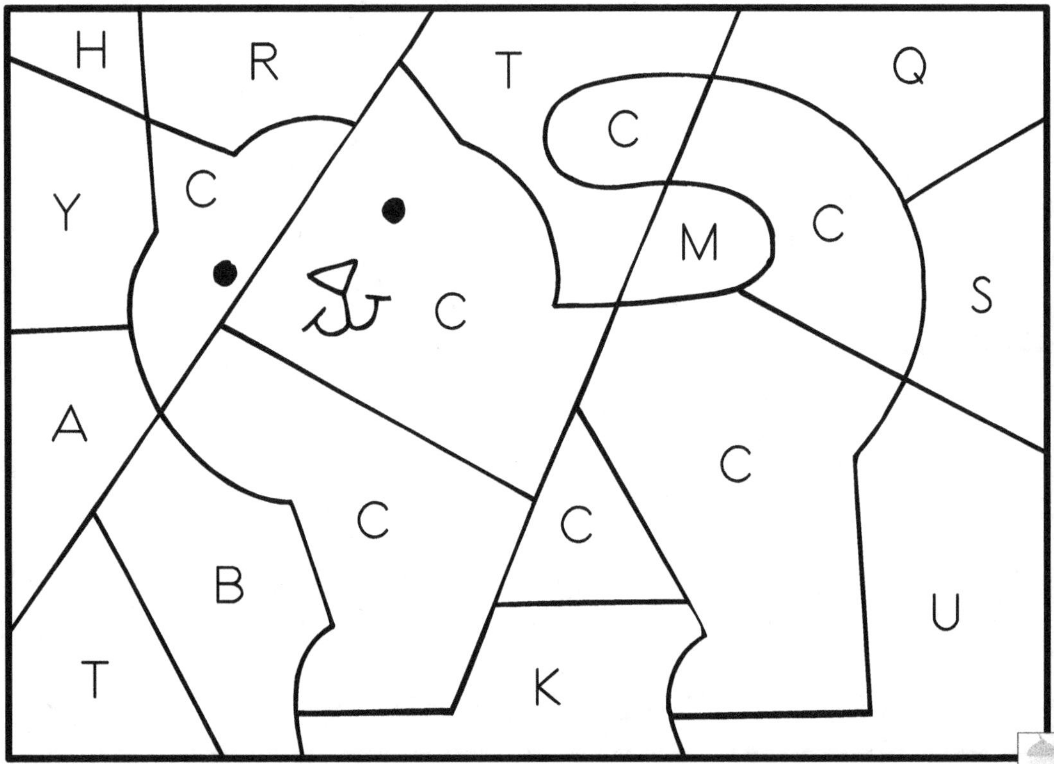

Color the **D** shapes yellow. Color all the other shapes green.

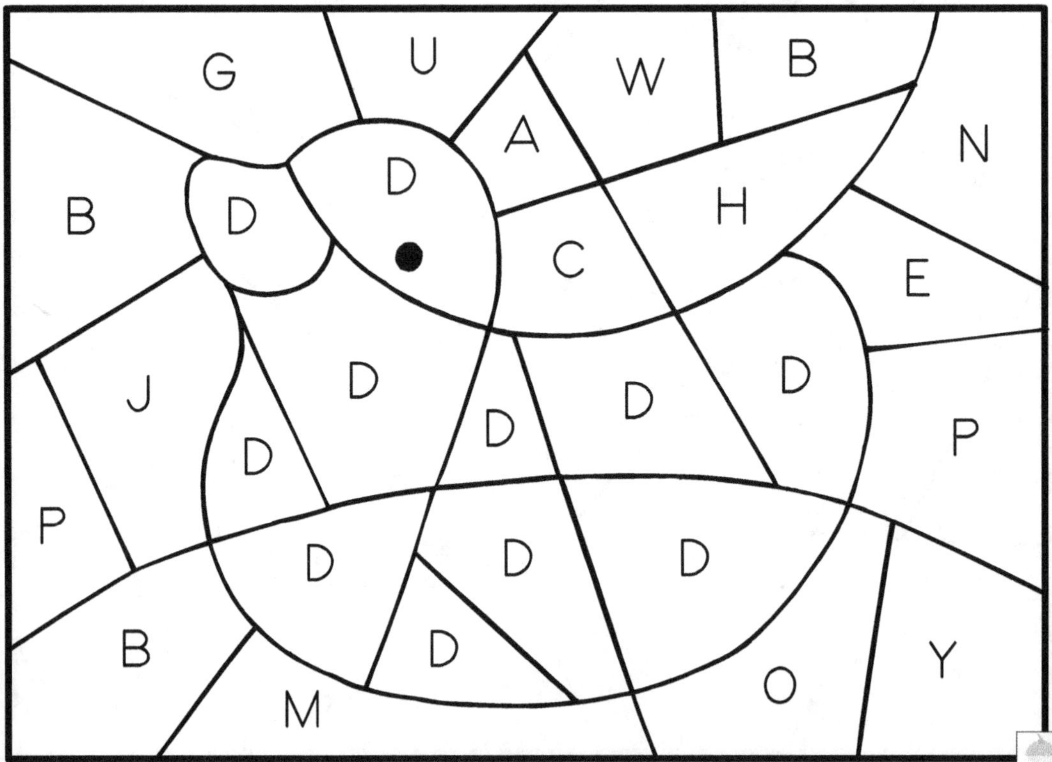

Color-By-Letter
Letters A-D

Color the **A** shapes yellow. Color the **B** shapes red.
Color the **C** shapes blue. Color the **D** shapes orange.

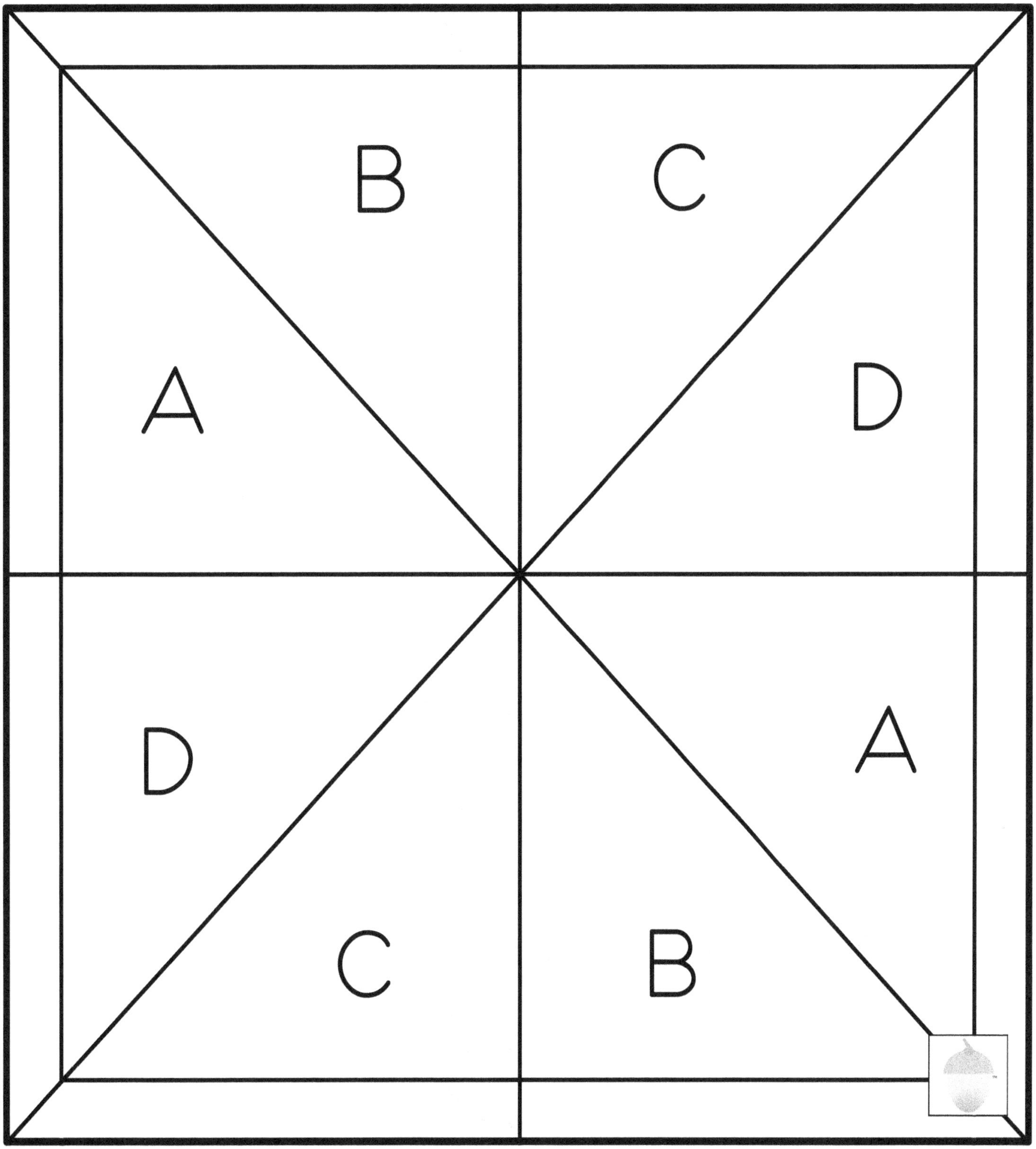

Alphabet Trail Game Board
Letters E-I

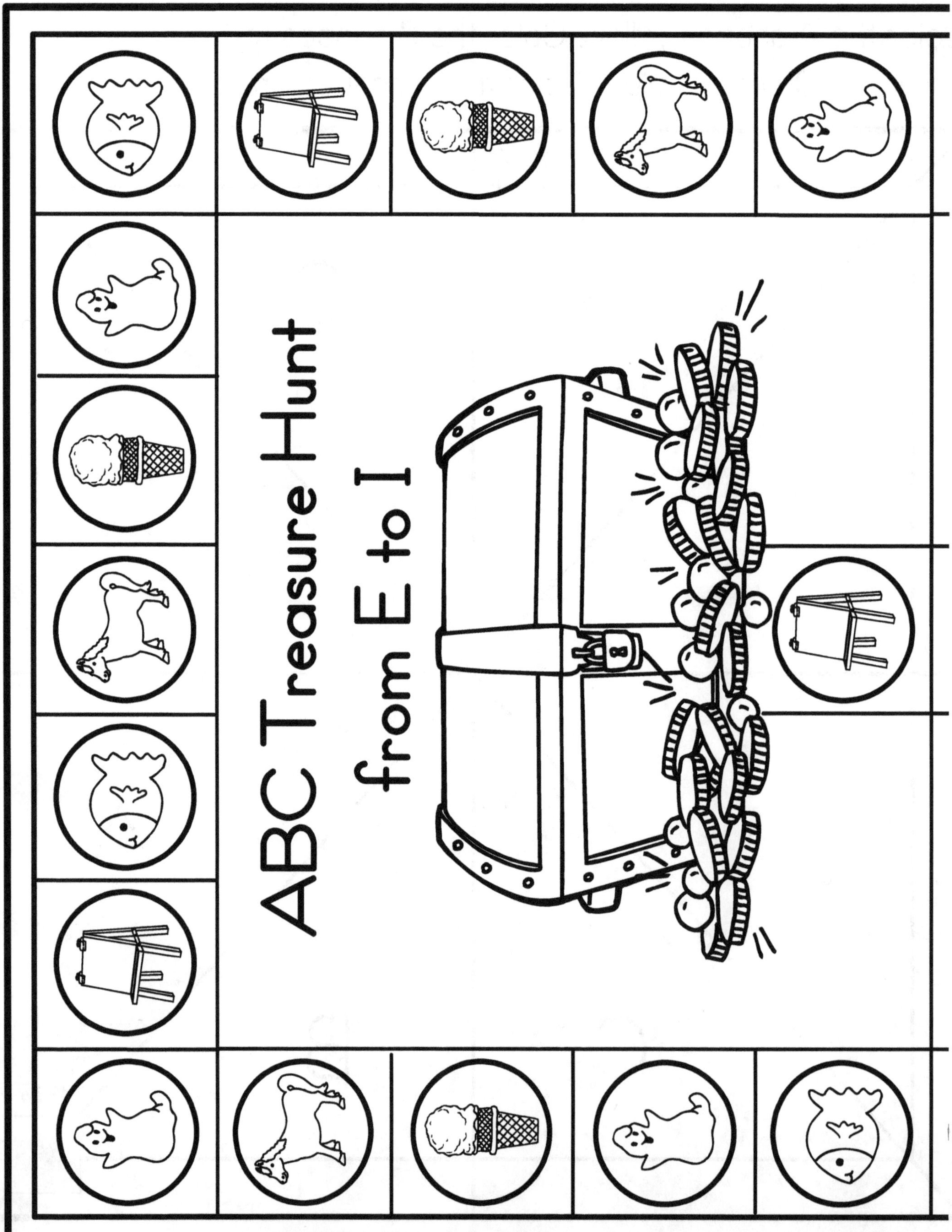

ABC Treasure Hunt from E to I

Alphabet Trail Game Board
Letters E-I

START

Spinner and Pawns
Letters E-I

Color each pawn a different color.

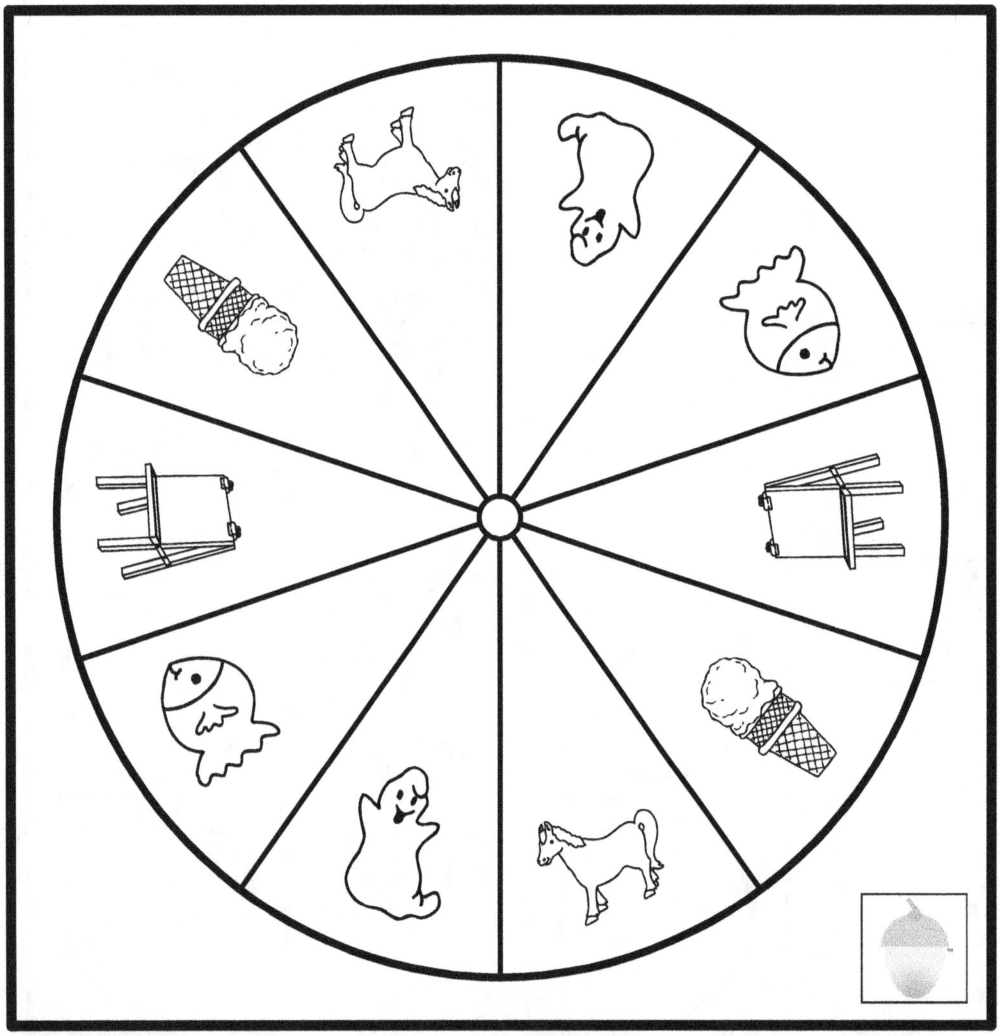

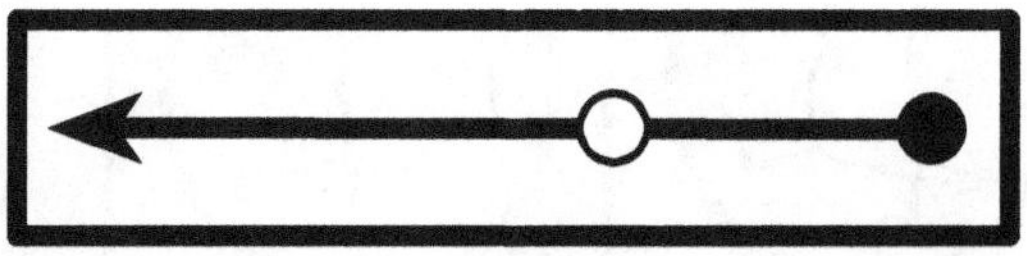

Color each pawn a different color.

Game Board Playing Cards
Letters E-I

| e | f | g | h | i |

| E | F | G | H | I |

Alphabet Bingo
Letters E-I

h	f	e
i	i	h
e	g	f
I	E	H
H	F	I
F	G	E

20   LAB20143P • ABC GAMES • 978-1-937257-59-0 • © 2014 Little Acorn Books™

Alphabet Bingo
Alphabet Pictures E-I

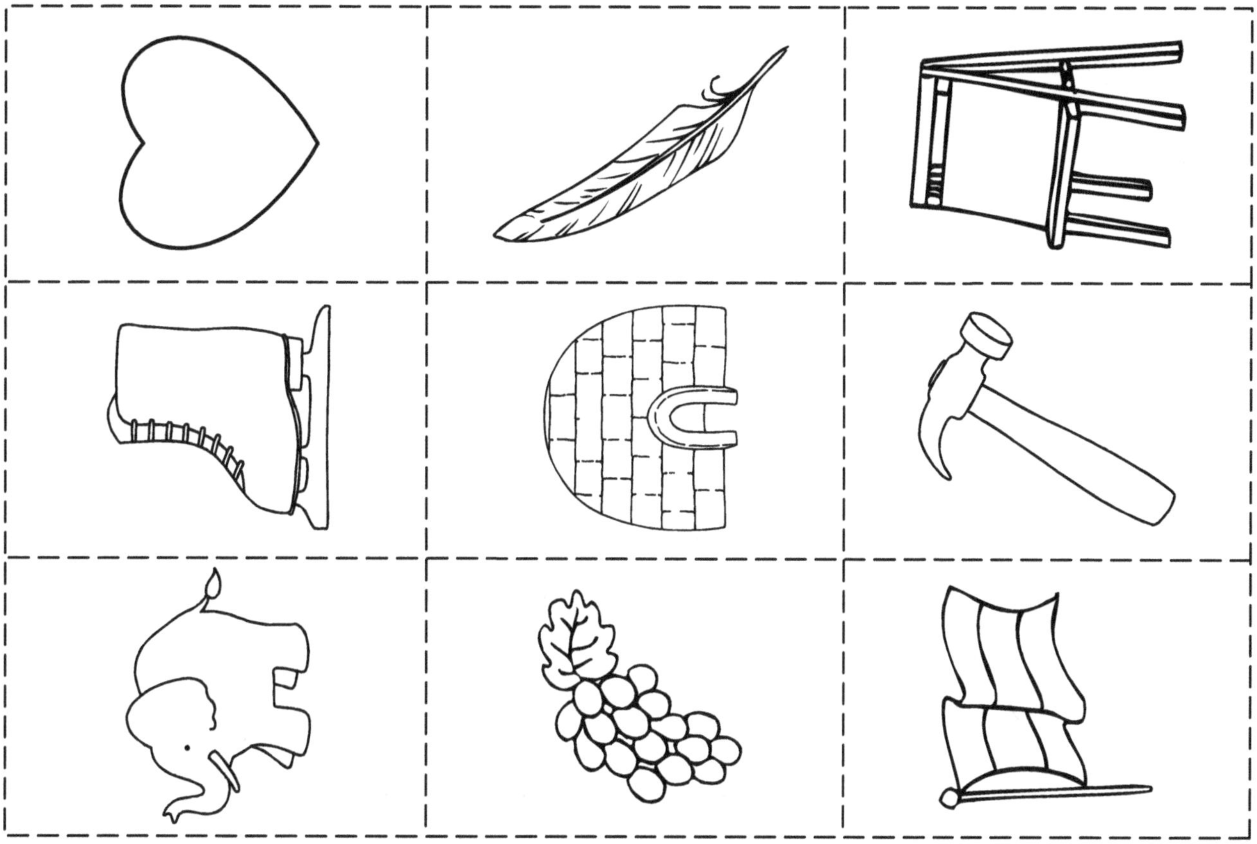

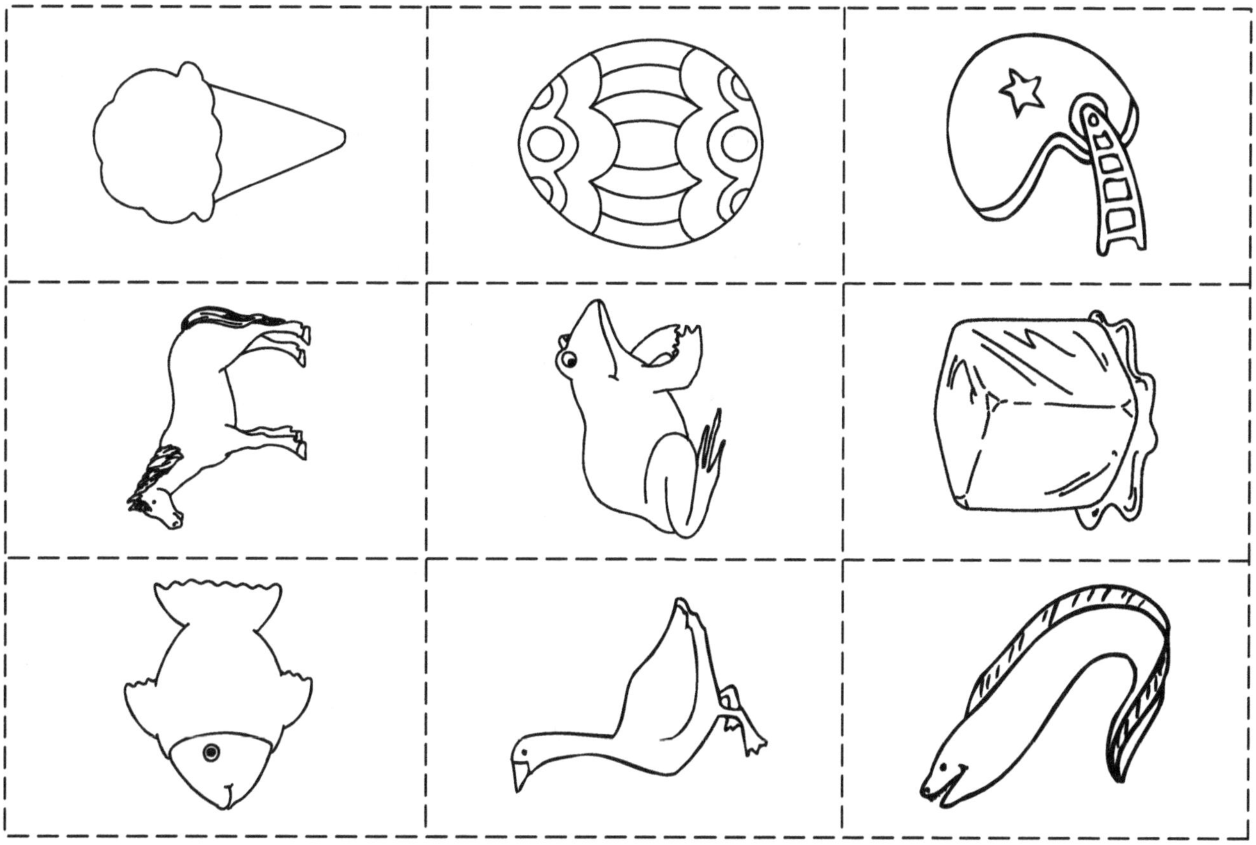

Alphabet Die

Letters E-I

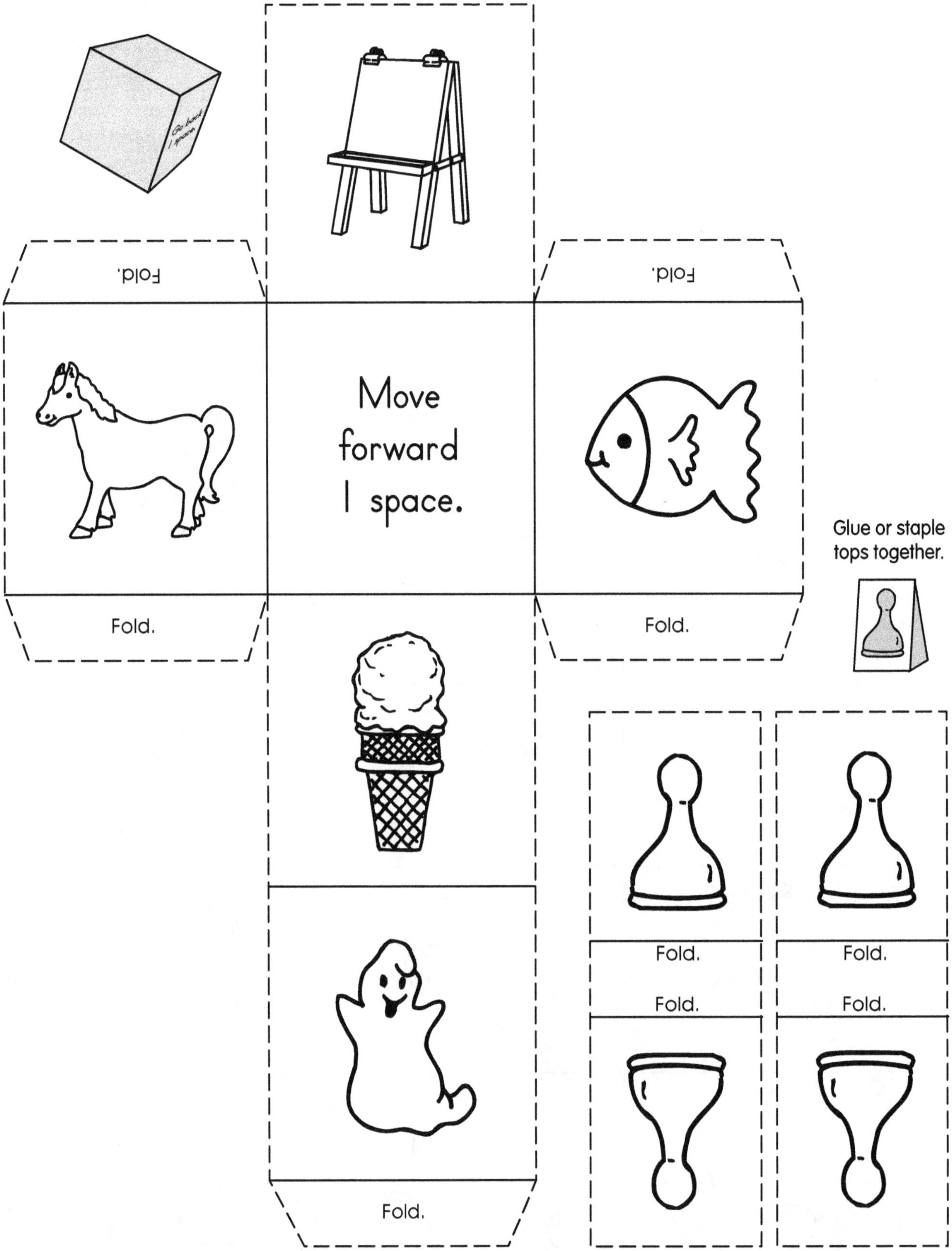
Fold.
Fold.
Move forward 1 space.
Fold.
Fold.
Fold.
Glue or staple tops together.
Fold.
Fold.
Fold.
Fold.

Color each pawn a different color.

LAB20143P • ABC GAMES • 978-1-937257-59-0 • © 2014 Little Acorn Books™

Color-By-Letter
Letters E and F

Color the **E** shapes white. Color all the other shapes yellow.

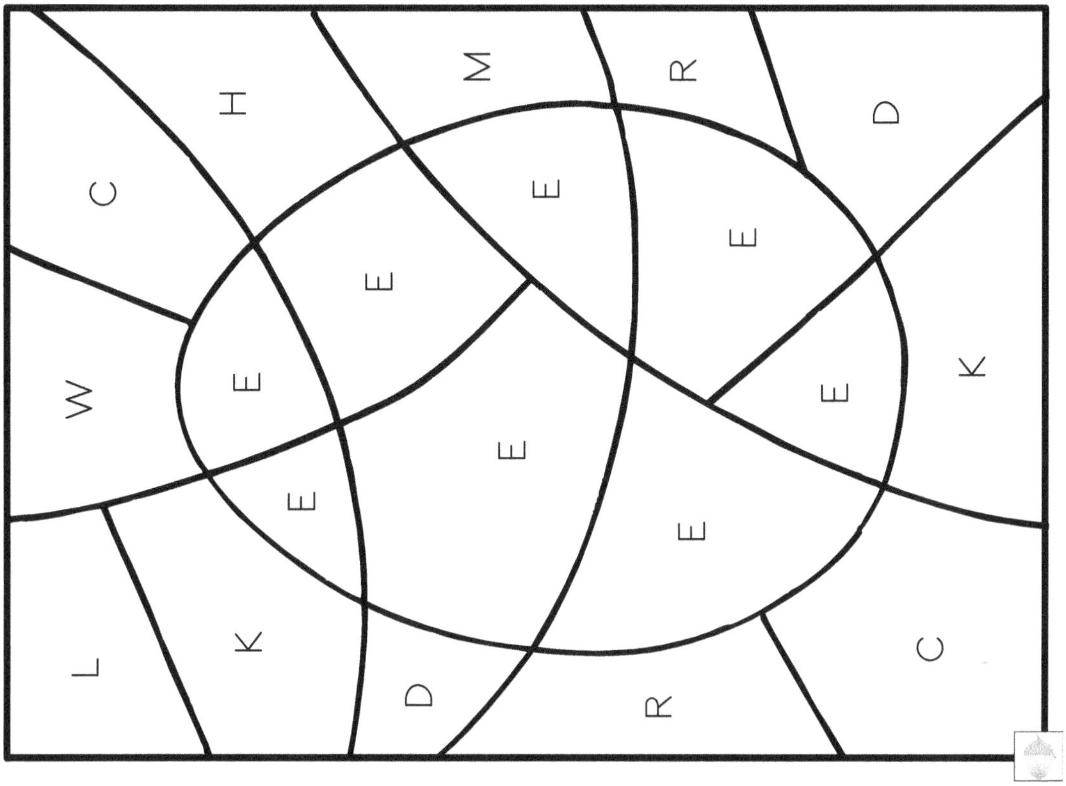

Color the **F** shapes green. Color all the other shapes orange.

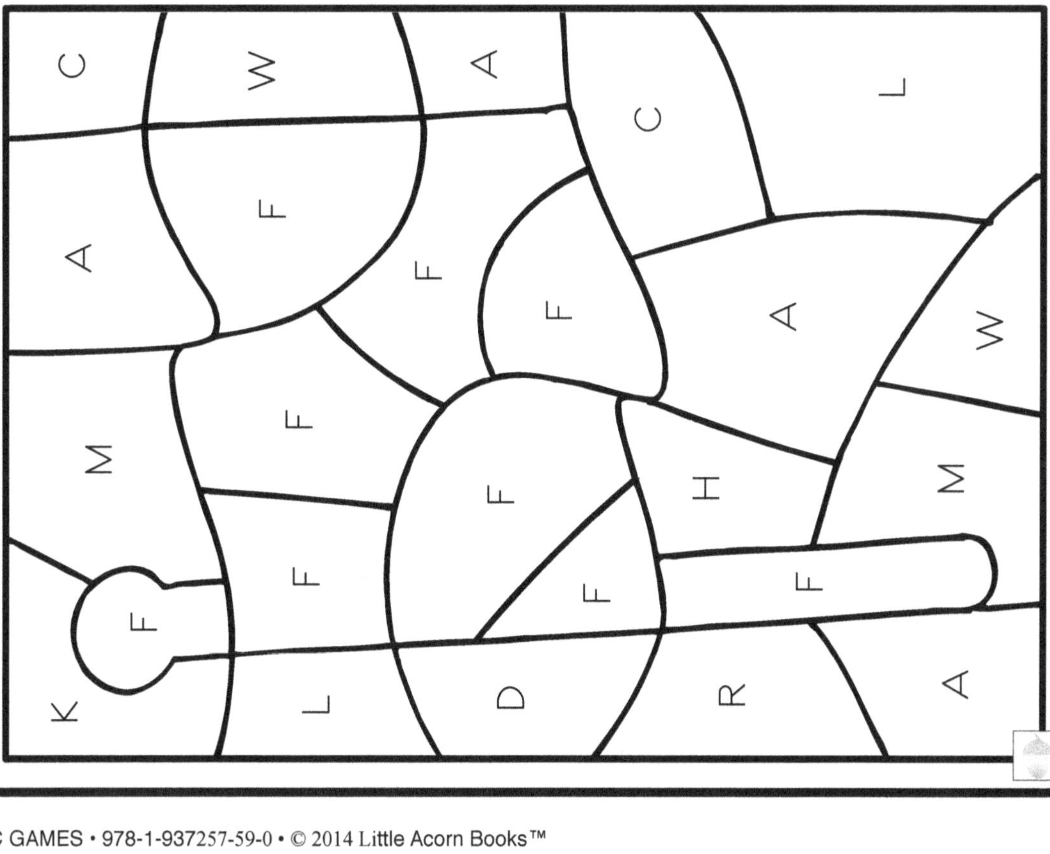

Color-By-Letter
Letters G and H

Color the **G** shapes white. Color all the other shapes blue.

Color the **H** shapes red. Color all the other shapes yellow.

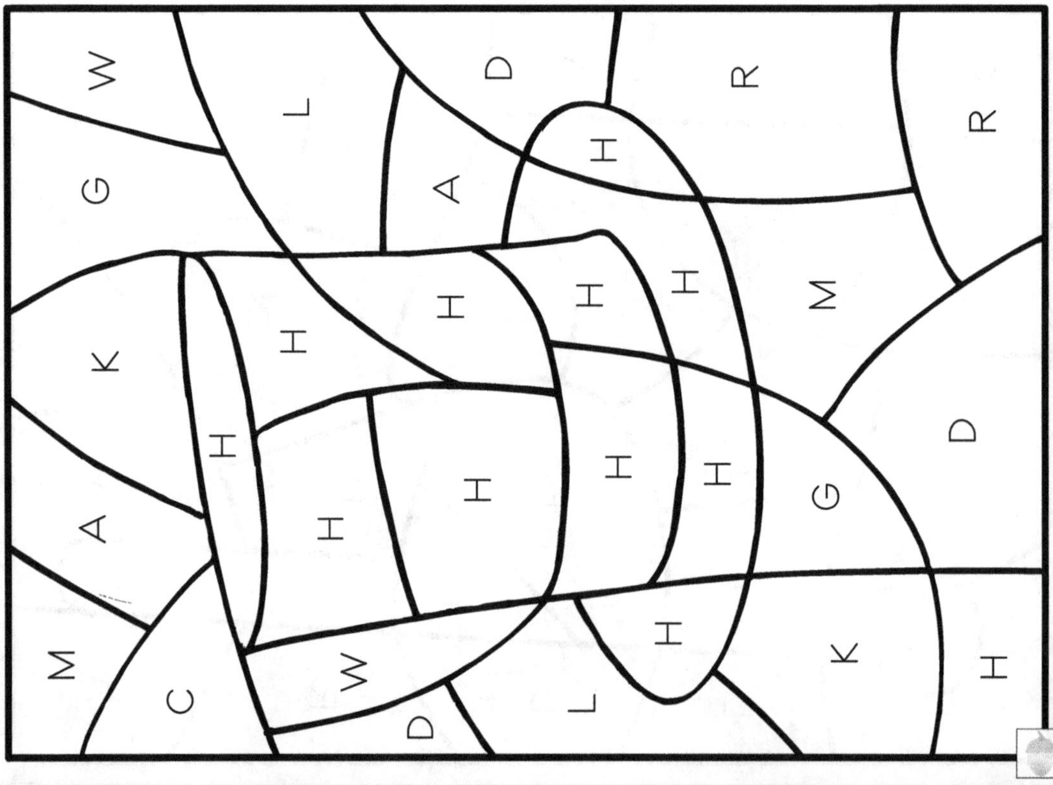

Color-By-Letter
Letter I

Color the I shapes white. Color all the other shapes red.

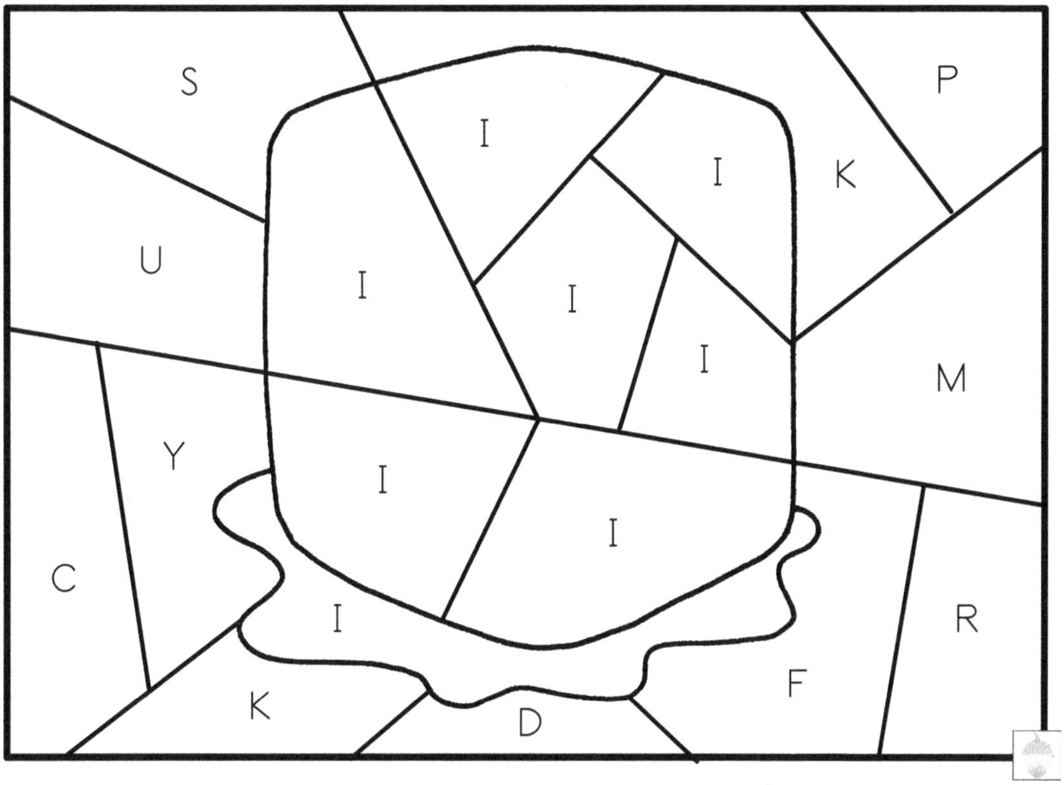

Color the I shapes blue. Color all the other shapes yellow.

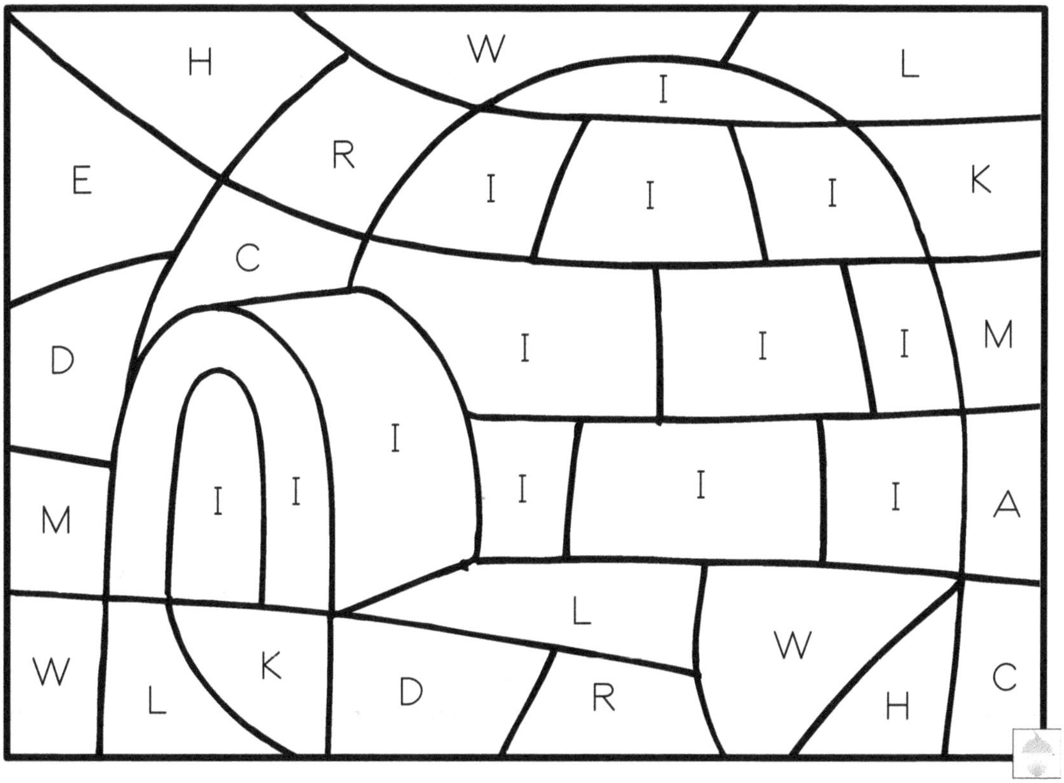

Color-By-Letter
Letters E-I

Color the **E** shapes yellow. Color the **F** shapes red.
Color the **G** shapes white. Color the **H** shapes purple.
Color the **I** shapes blue.

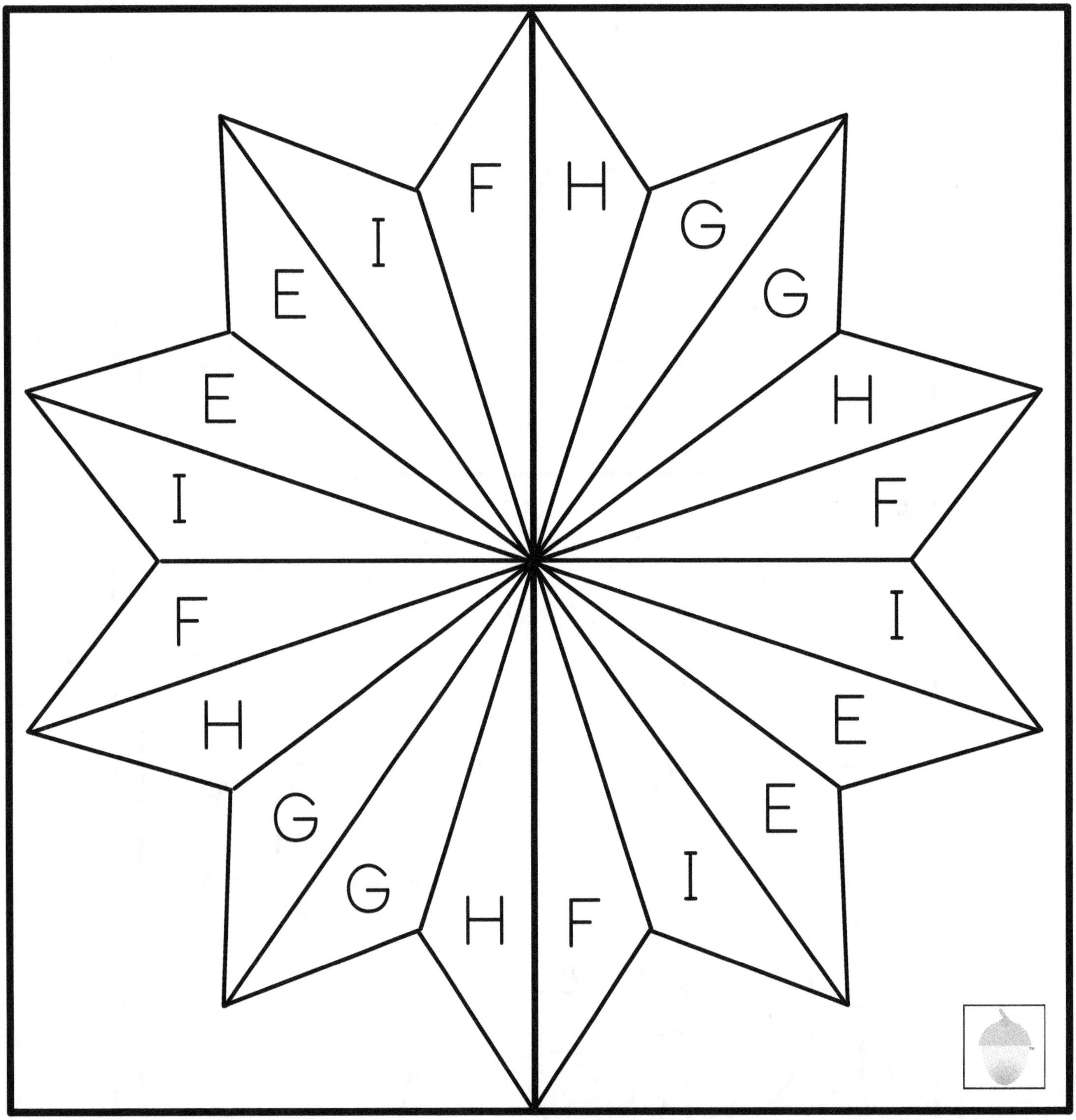

Alphabet Trail Game Board
Letters J-M

Follow the Alphabet Trail from J to M

START → THE END

Alphabet Trail Game Board
Letters J-M

Spinner and Pawns
Letters J-M

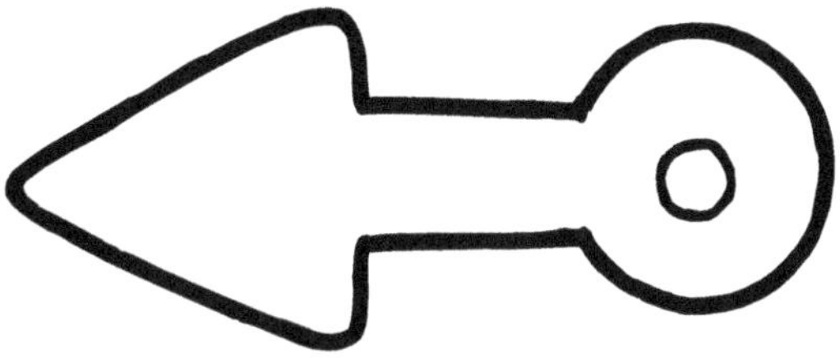

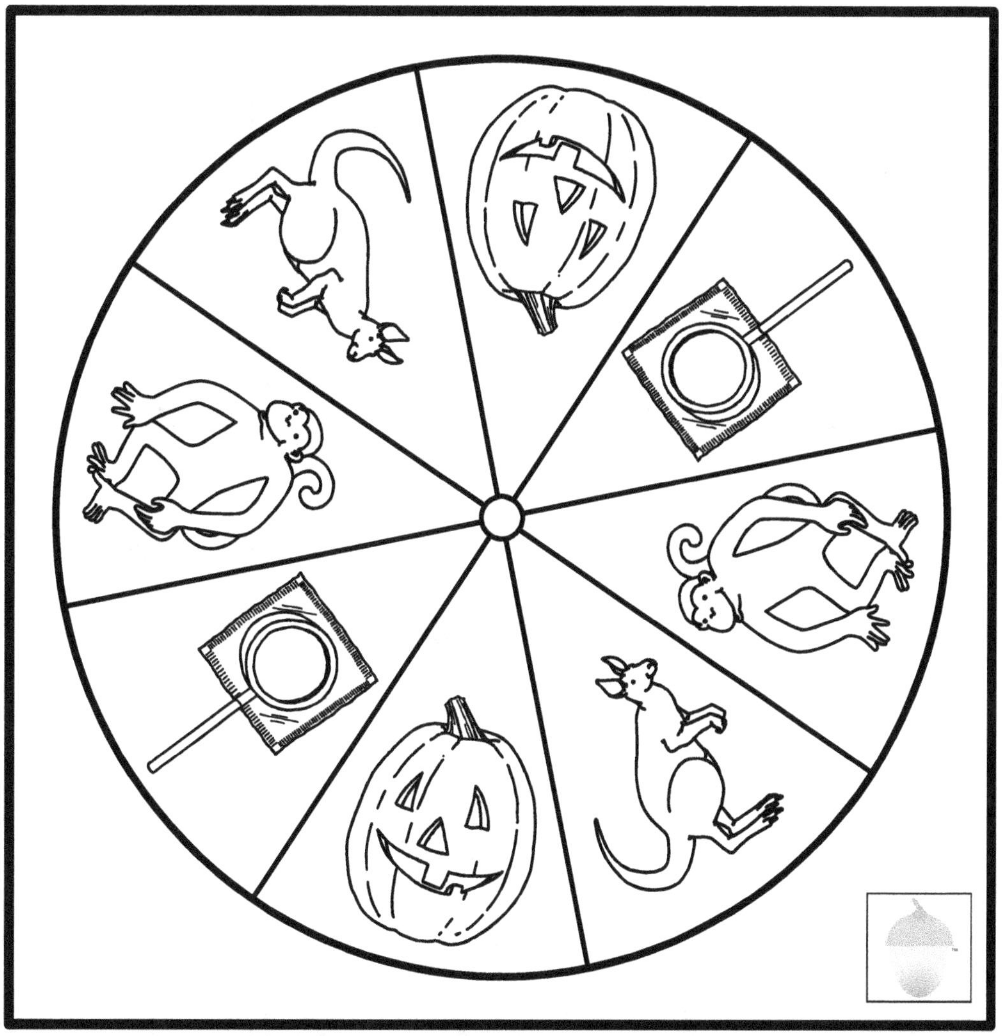

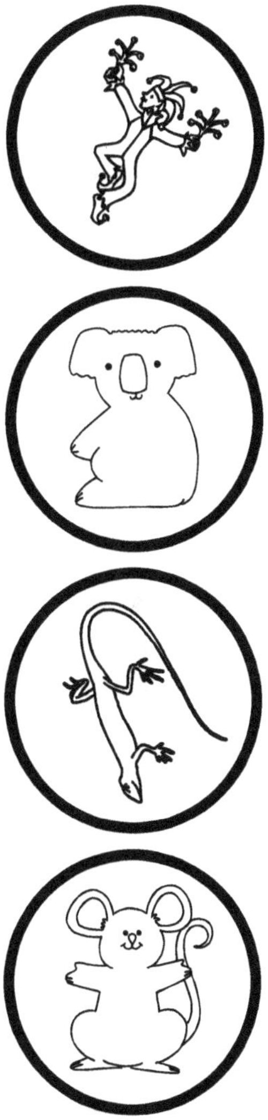

Color each pawn a different color.

Game Board Playing Cards
Letters J-M

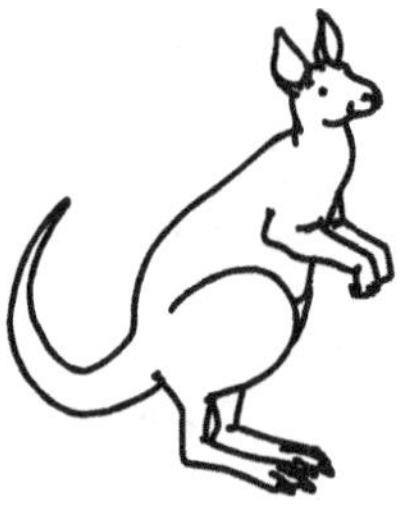	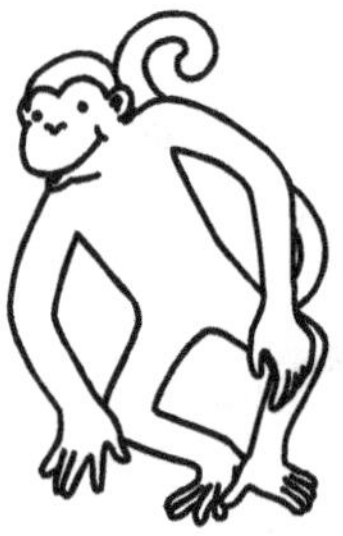	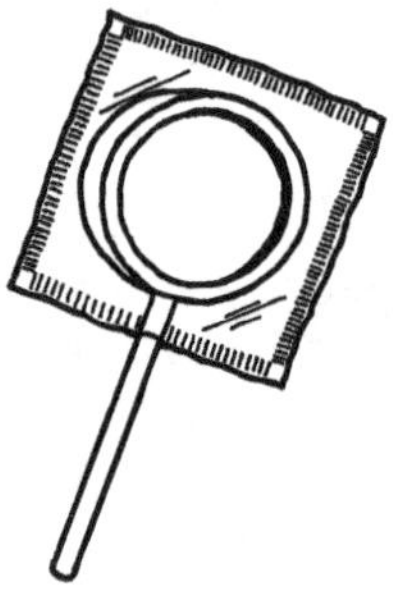	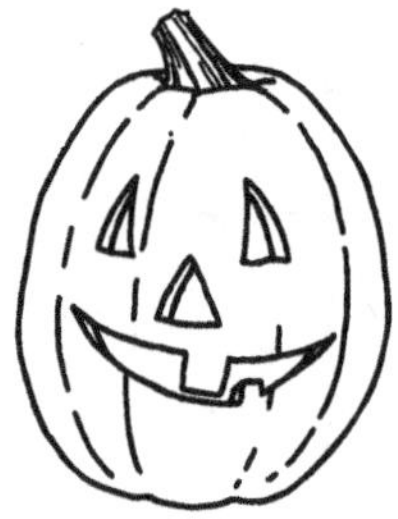	Move forward 1 space.
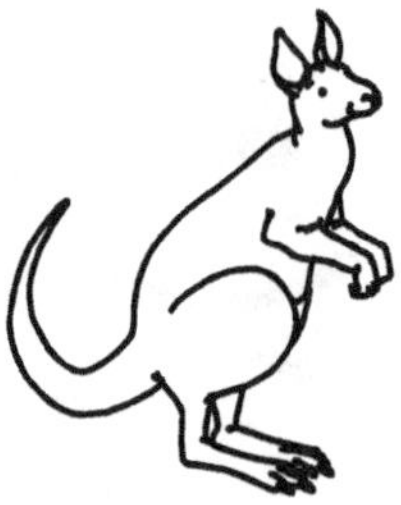	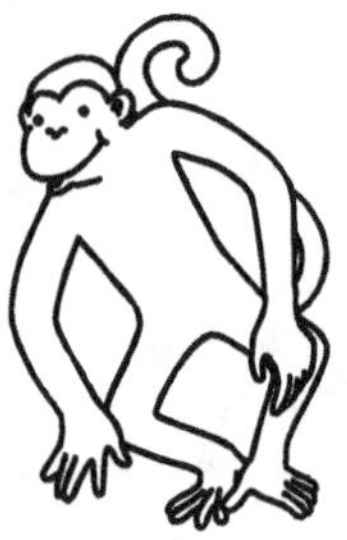	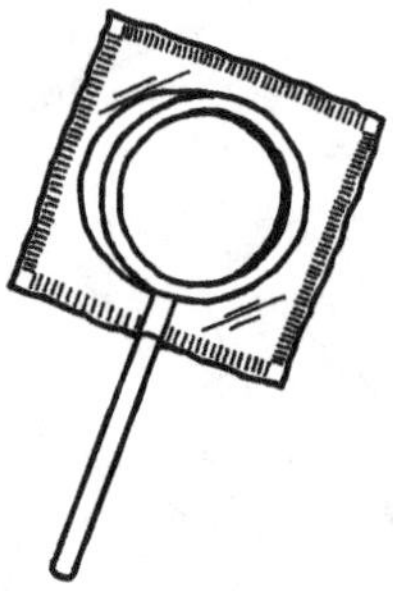	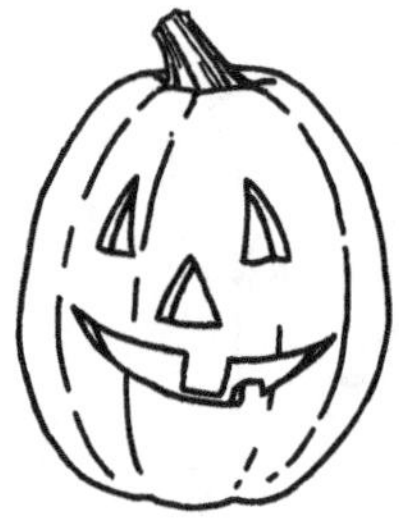	Move back 1 space.
j	k	l	m	Move forward 1 space.
J	K	L	M	Move back 1 space.

Alphabet Bingo
Alphabet Pictures J-M

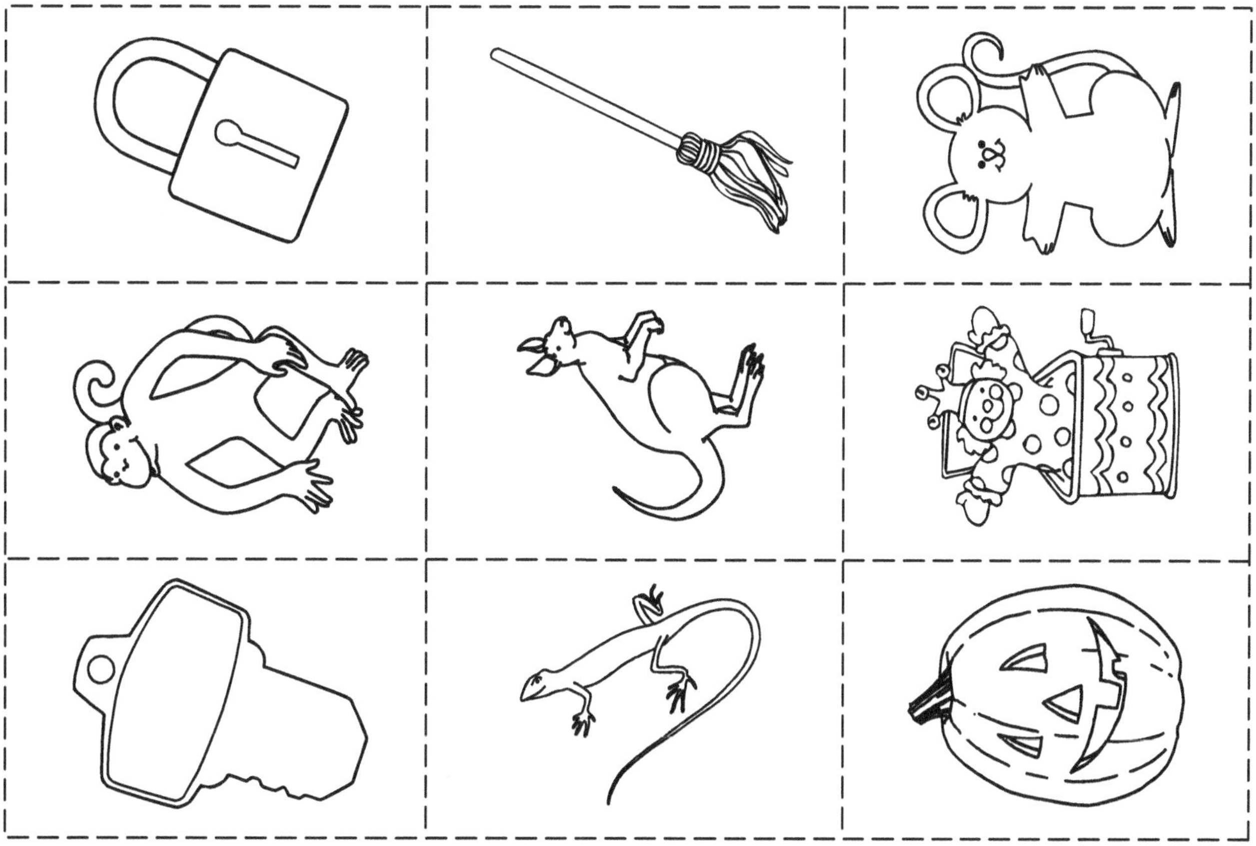

Alphabet Bingo
Letters J-M

m	k	m
l	j	m
j	l	k
L	M	M
M	K	J
K	L	J

Alphabet Die

Letters J-M

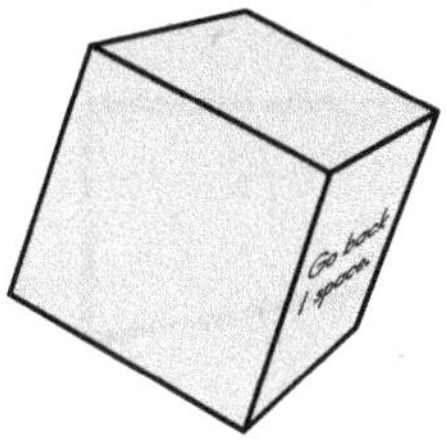

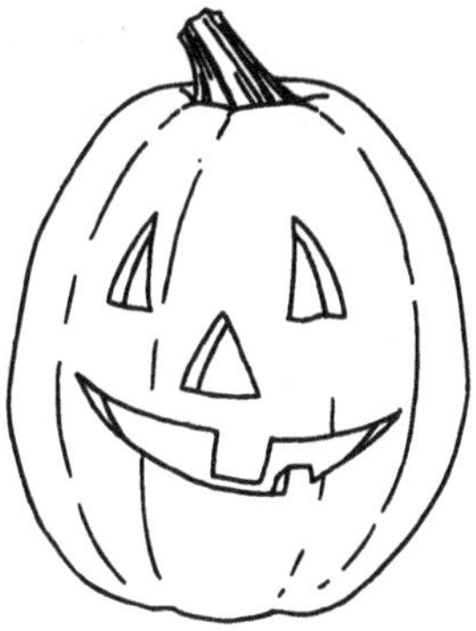

Fold.

Fold.

Move forward 1 space.

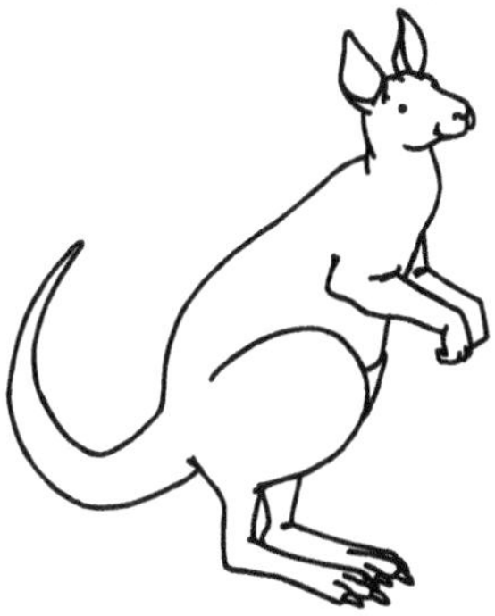

Go back 1 space.

Glue or staple tops together.

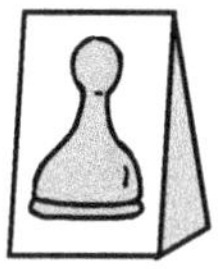

Fold.

Fold.

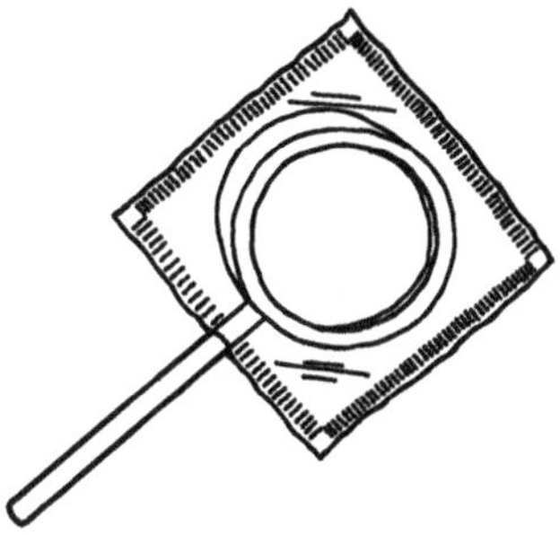

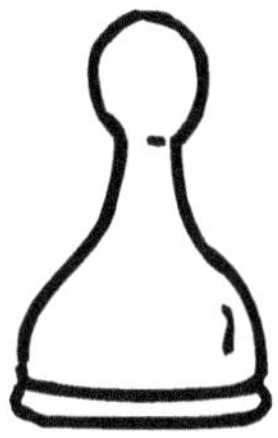

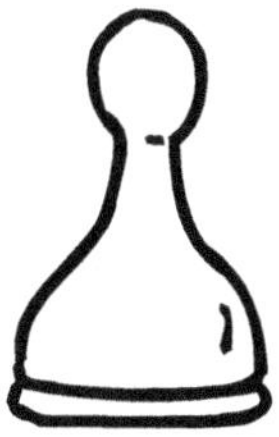

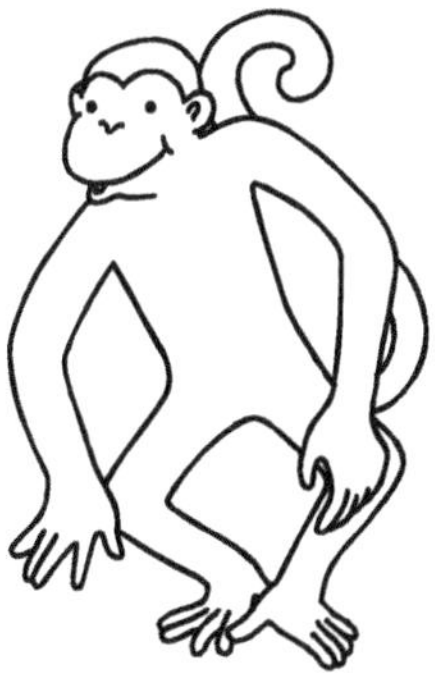

Fold.

Fold.

Fold.

Fold.

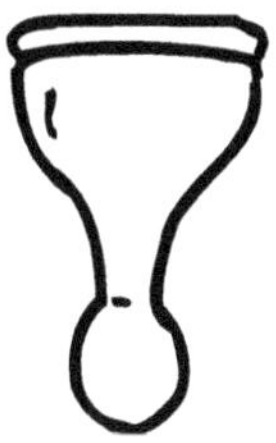

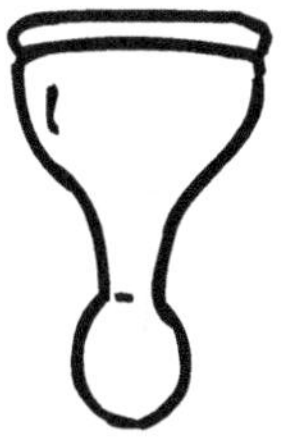

Fold.

Color each pawn a different color.

Color-By-Letter
Letters J and K

Color the **J** shapes red. Color all the other shapes orange.

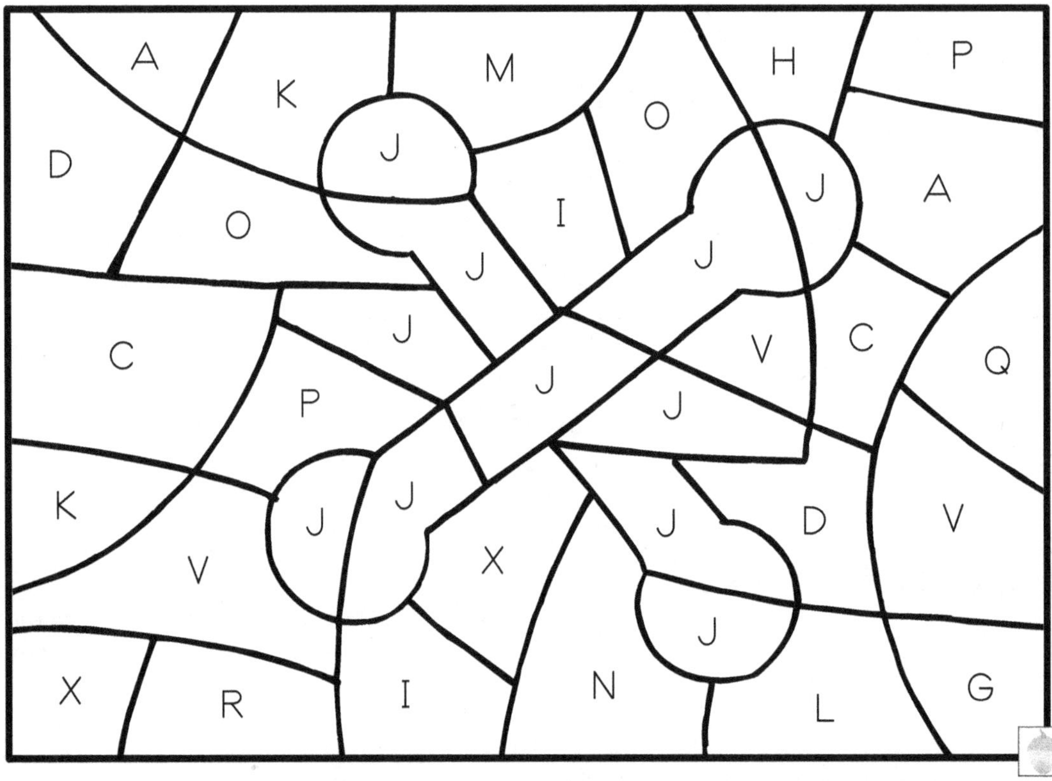

Color the **K** shapes red. Color all the other shapes yellow.

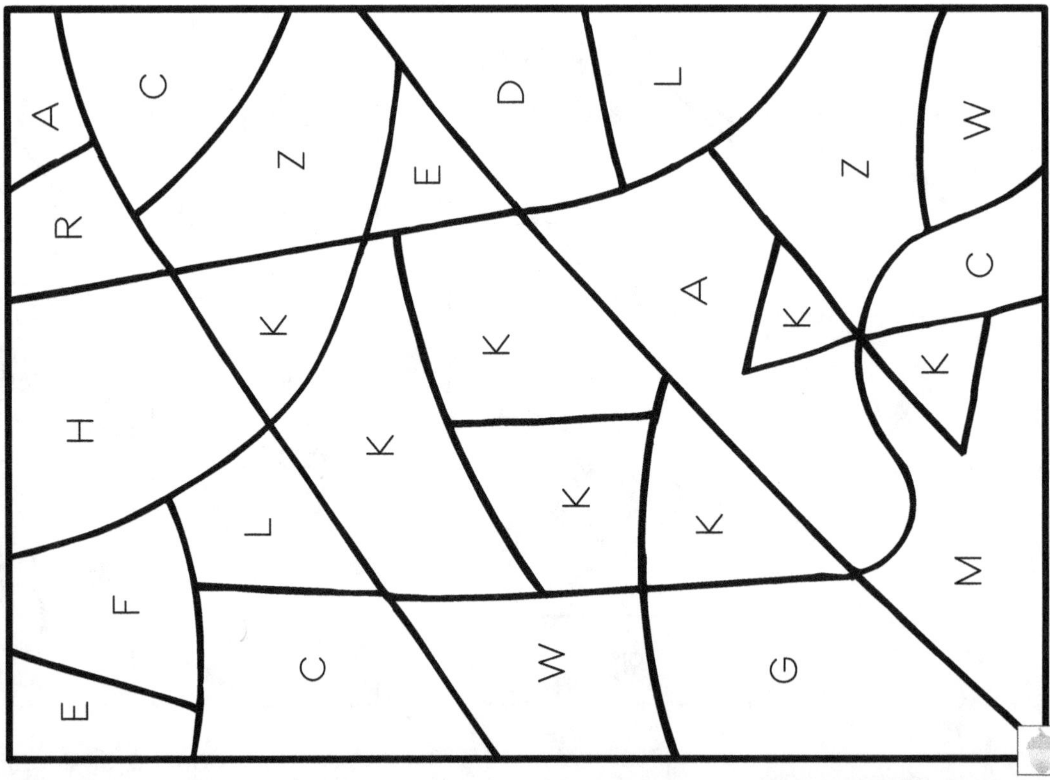

Color-By-Letter
Letters L and M

Color the L shapes yellow. Color all the other shapes blue.

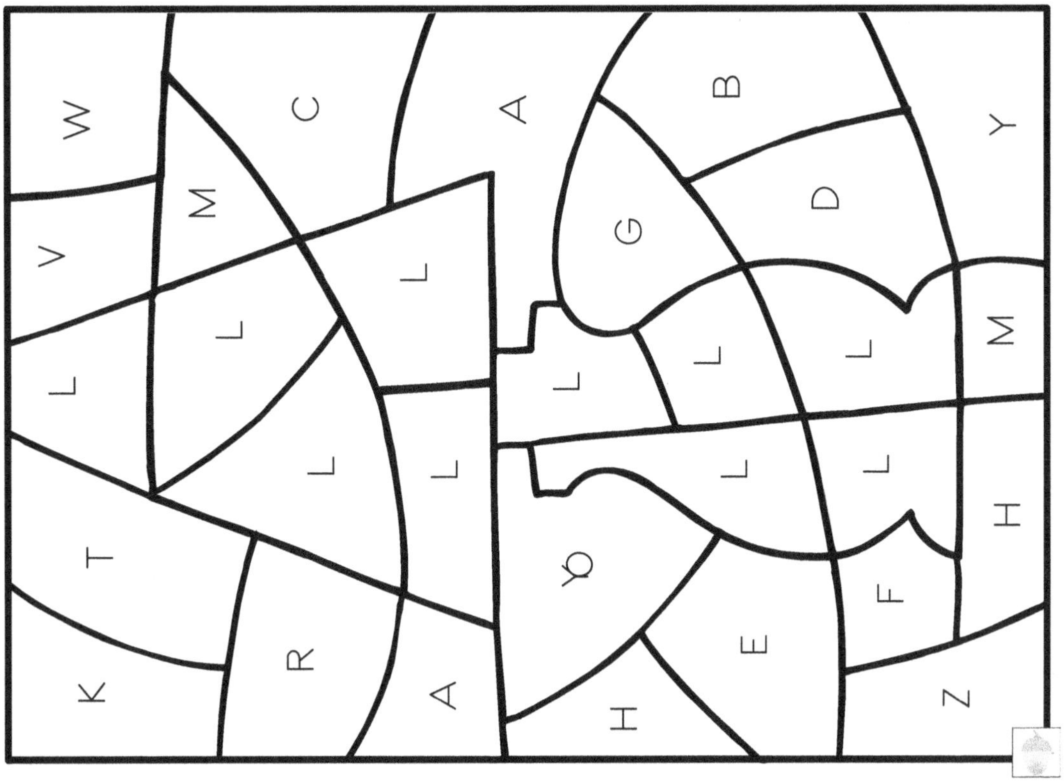

Color the M shapes brown. Color all the other shapes green.

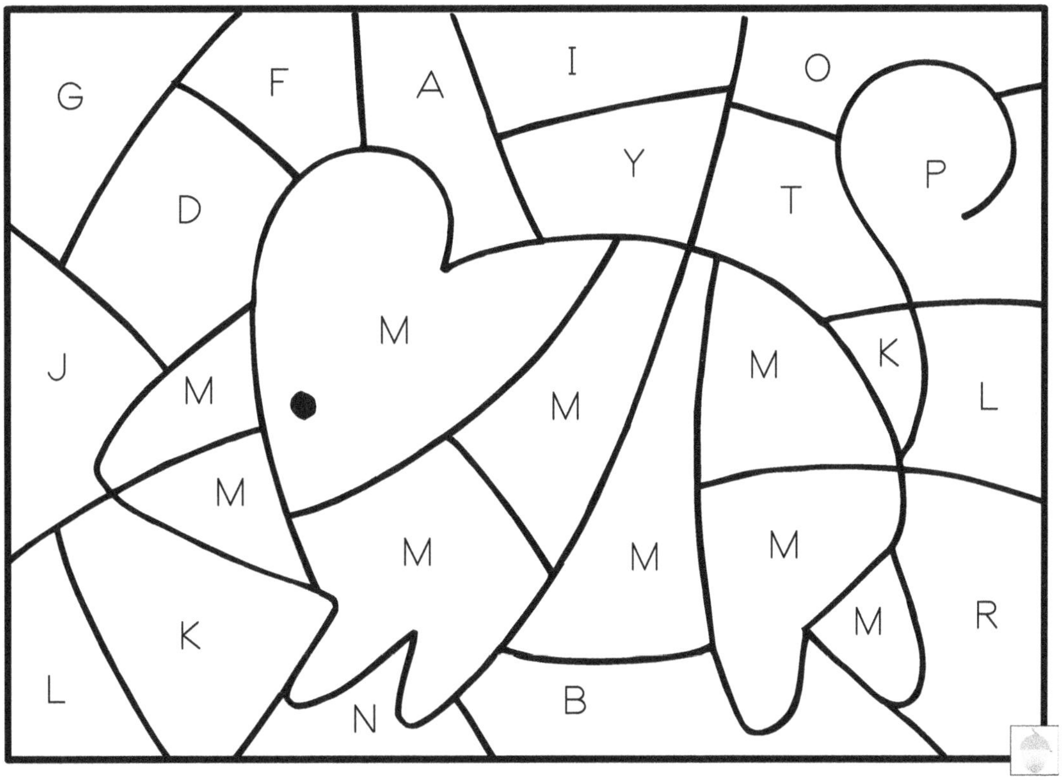

Color-By-Letter
Letters J-M

Color the **J** shapes yellow. Color the **K** shapes orange.
Color the **L** shapes pink. Color the **M** shapes purple.

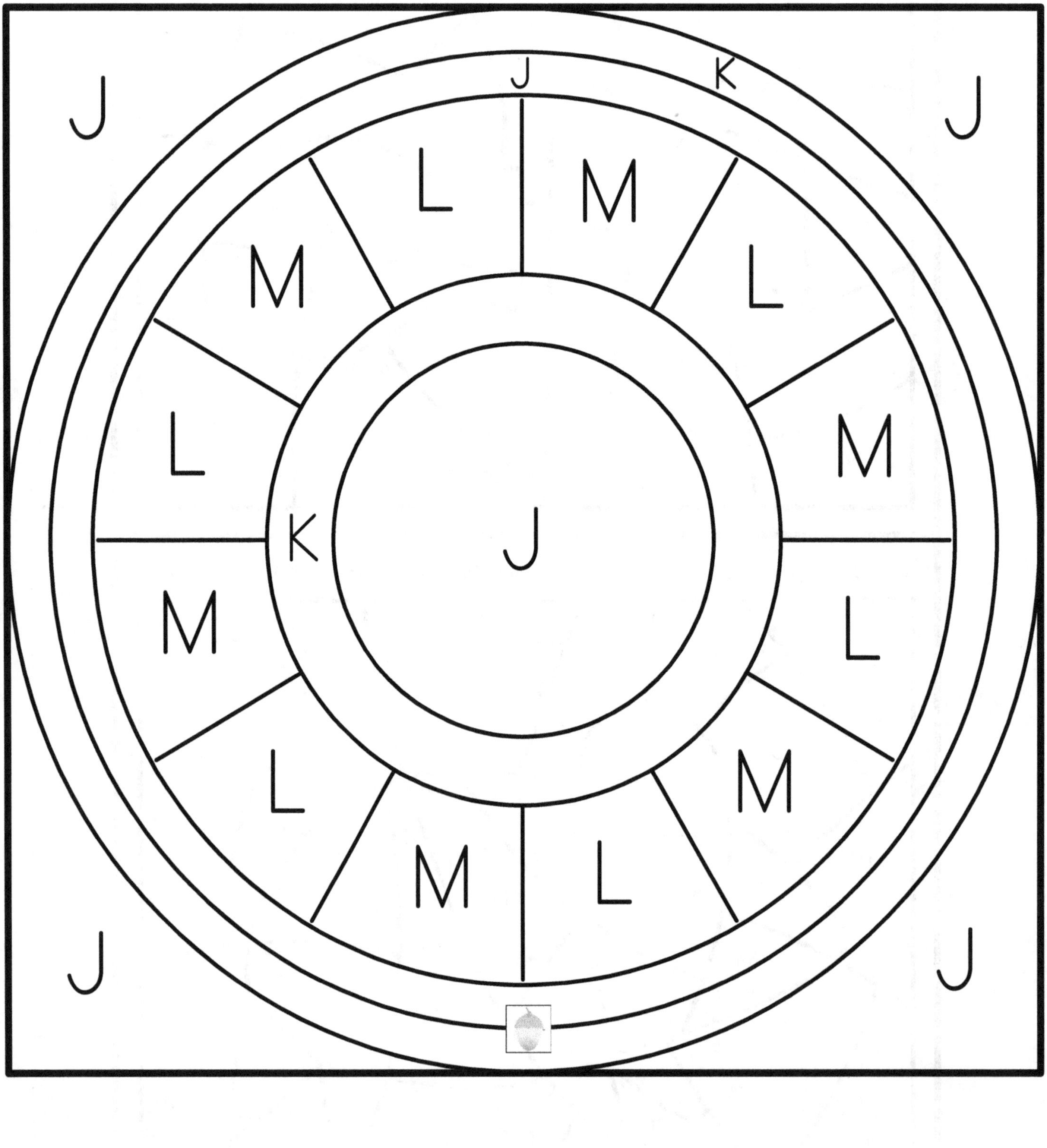

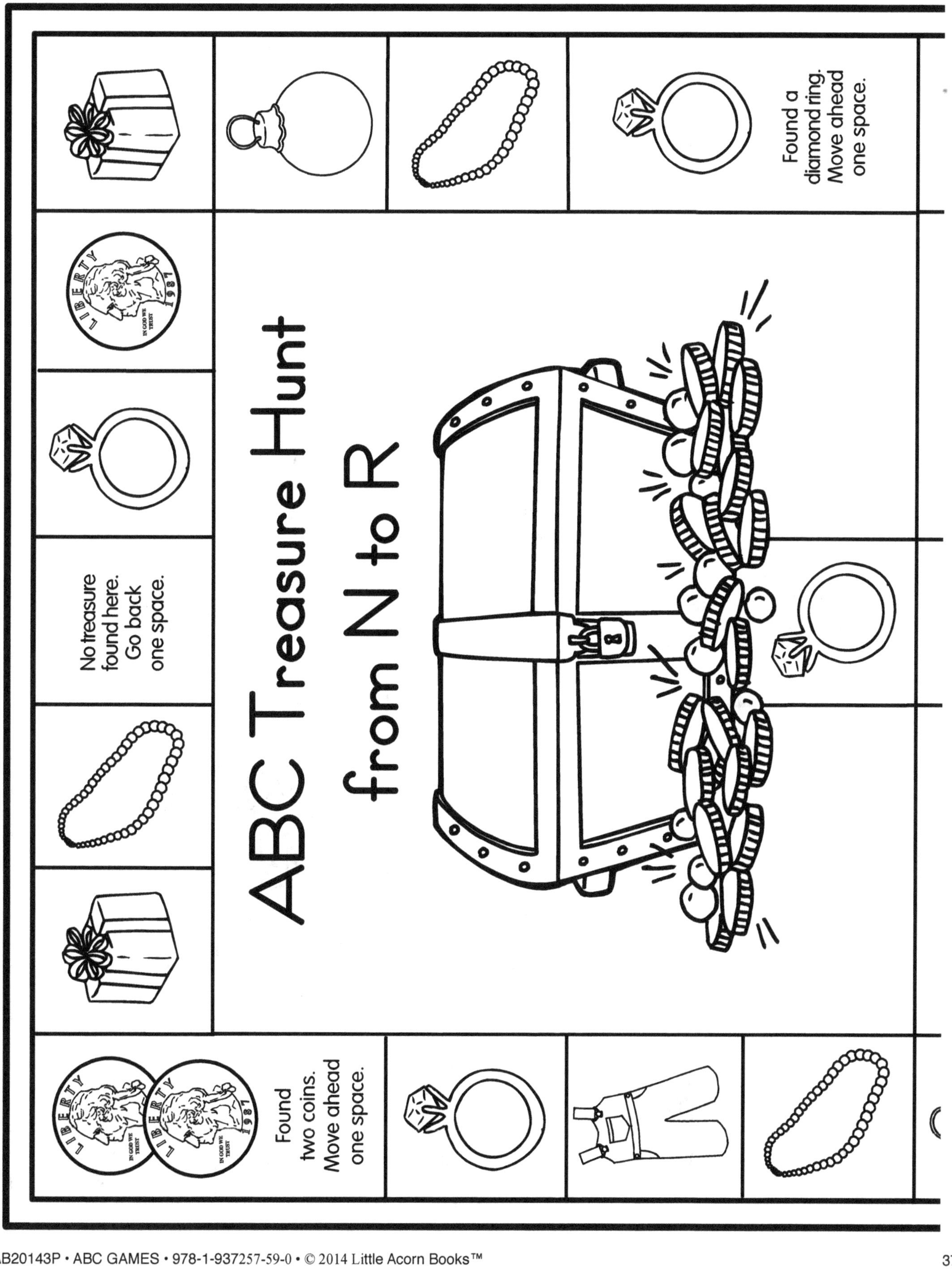

Alphabet Trail Game Board
Letters N-R

ABC Treasure Hunt from N to R

- Found a diamond ring. Move ahead one space.
- No treasure found here. Go back one space.
- Found two coins. Move ahead one space.

Alphabet Trail Game Board
Letters N-R

START

Spinner and Pawns
Letters N-R

Color each pawn a different color.

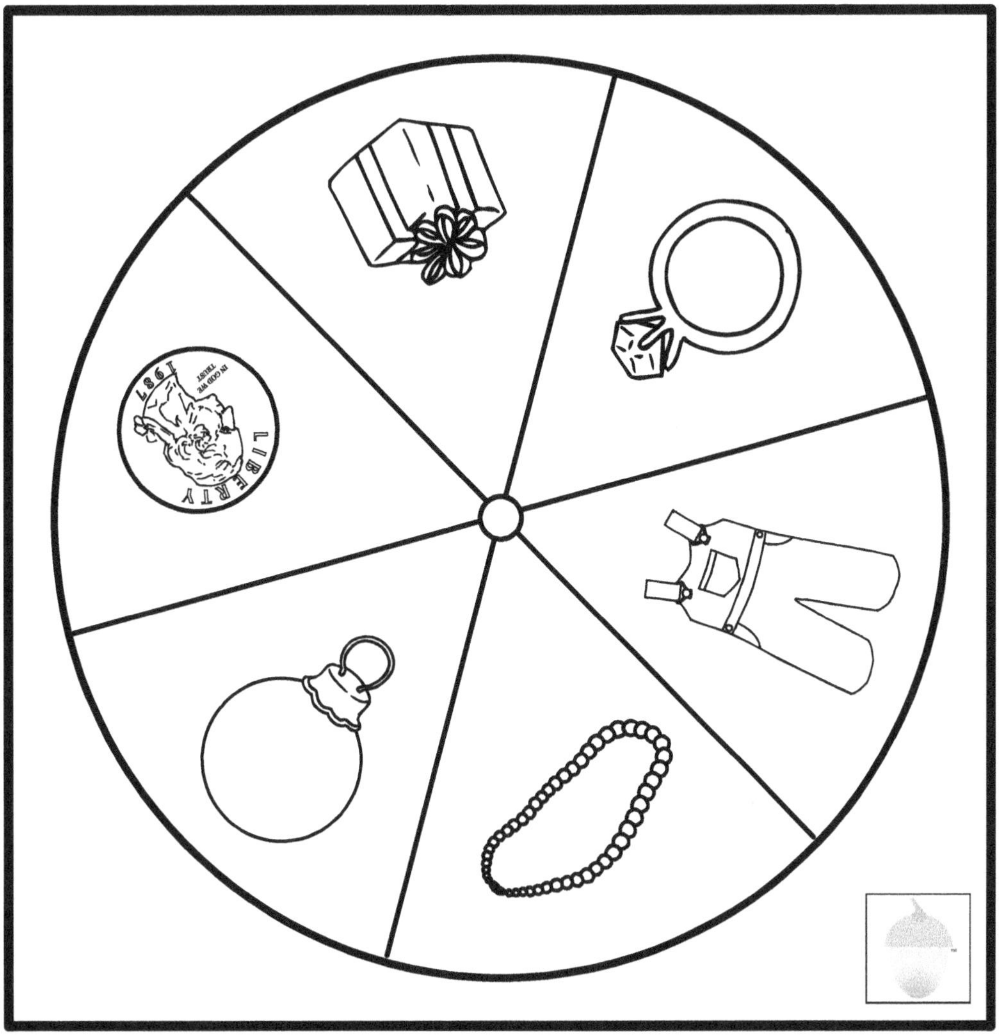

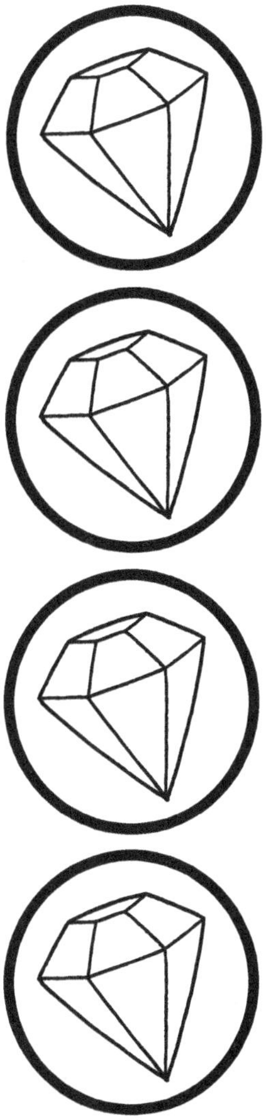

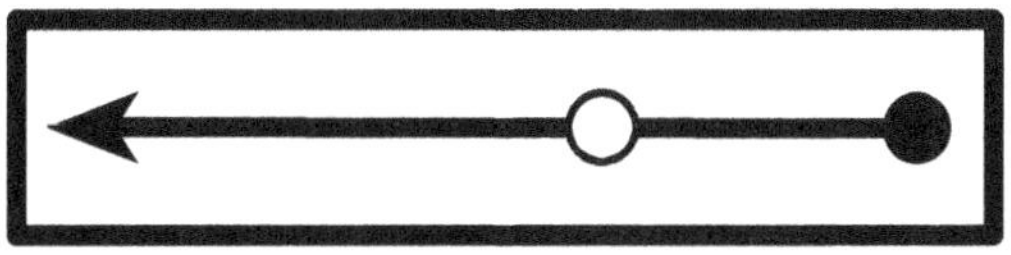

Color each pawn a different color.

Game Board Playing Cards
Letters N-R

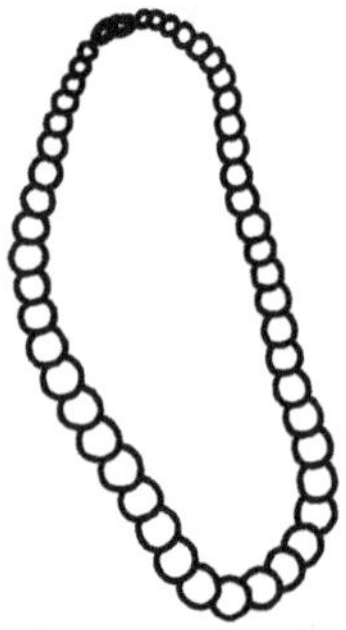

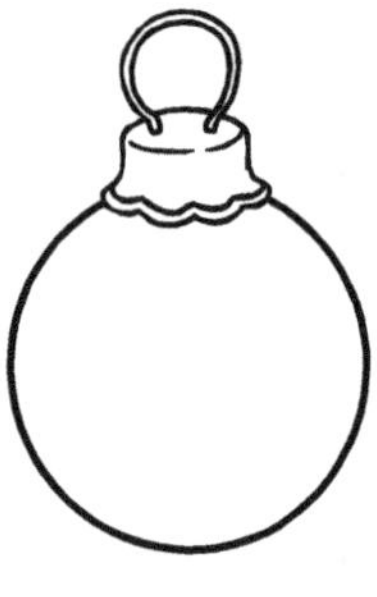

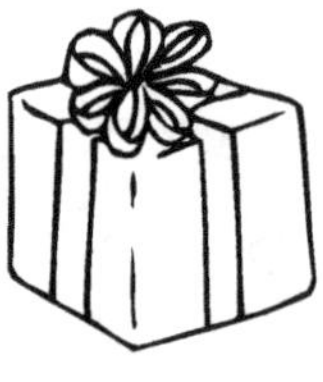

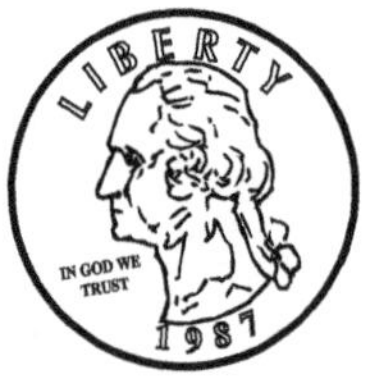

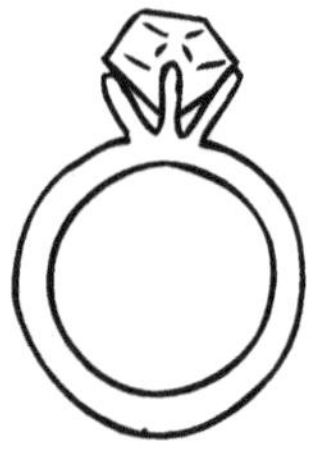

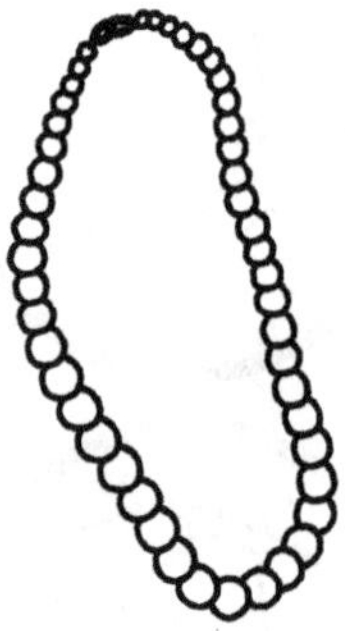

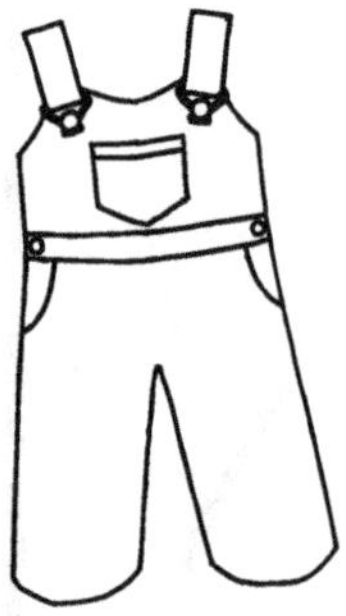

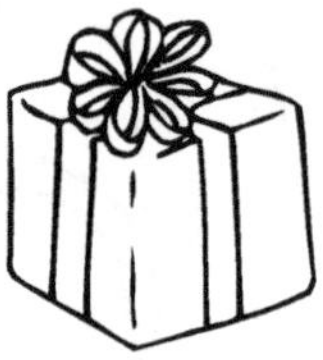

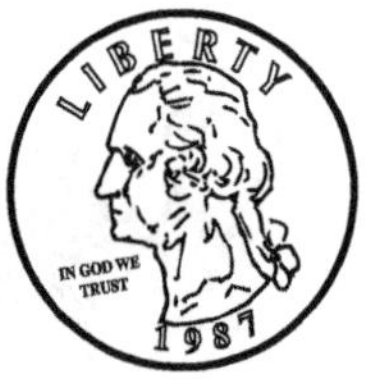

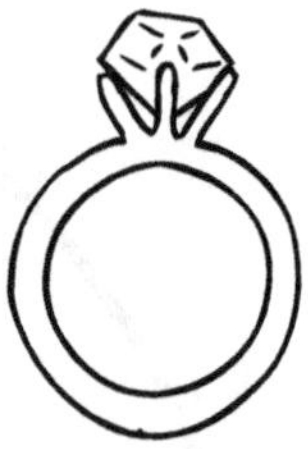

n o p q r

N O P Q R

Alphabet Bingo
Alphabet Pictures N-R

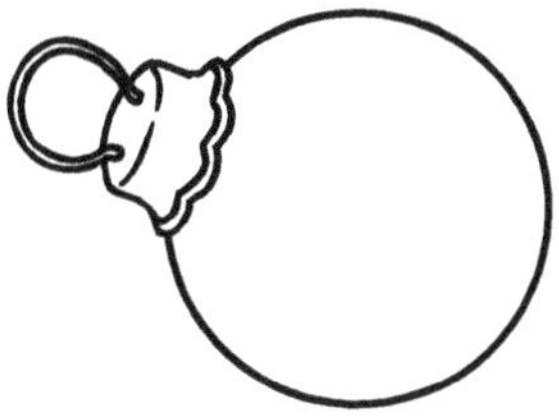

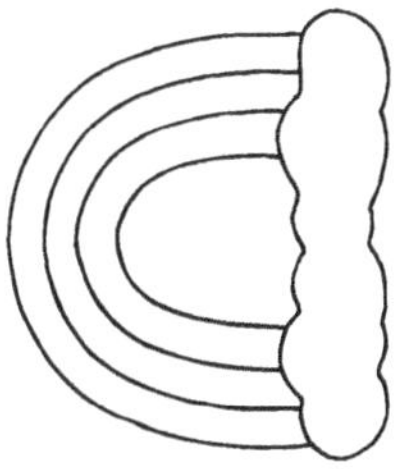

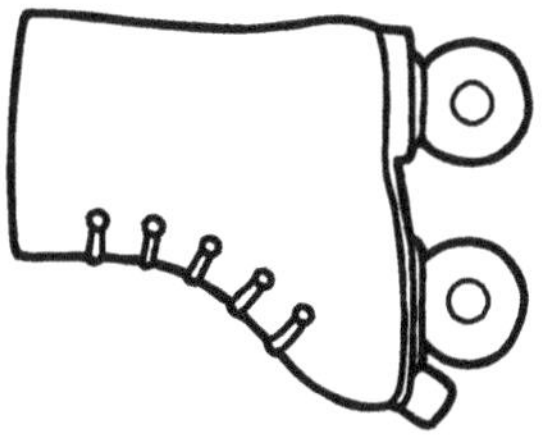

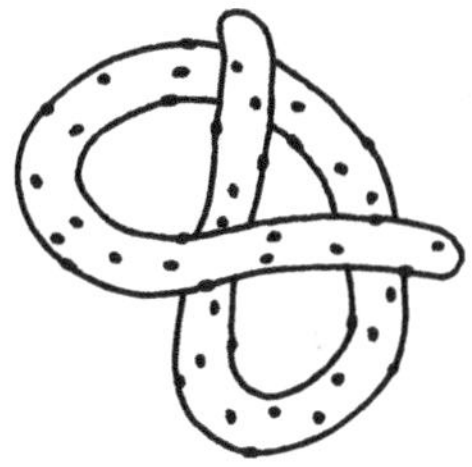

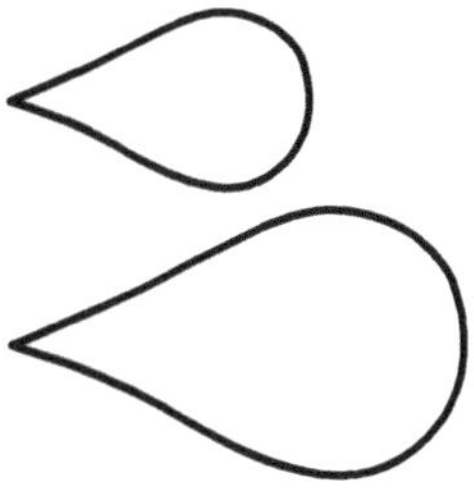

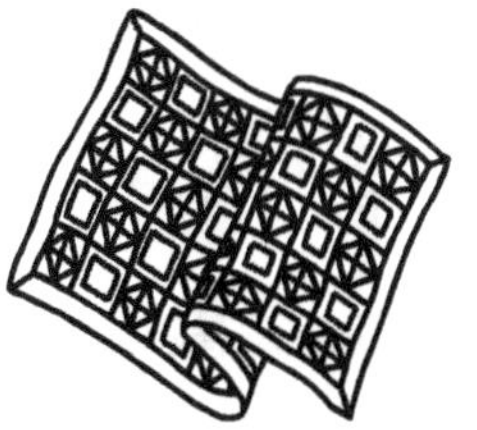

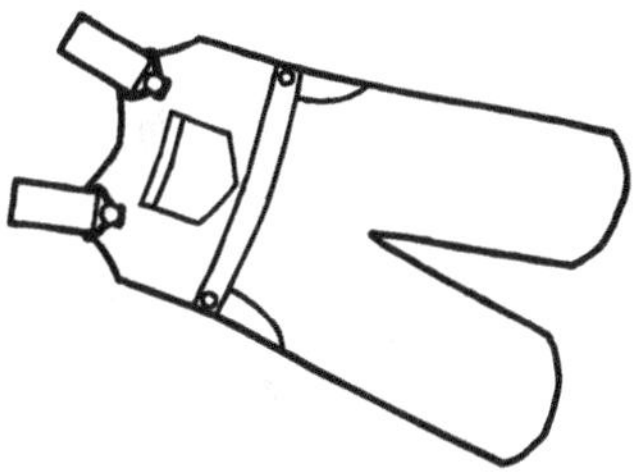

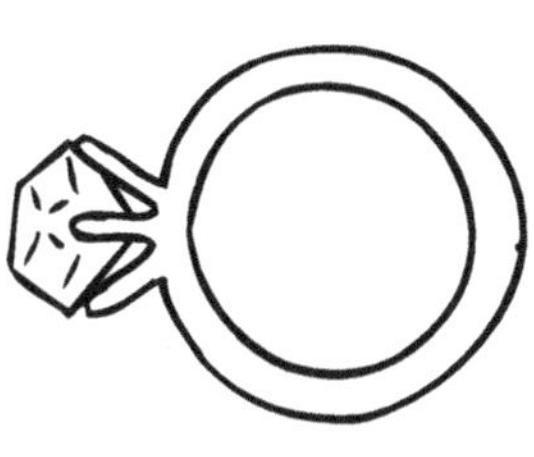

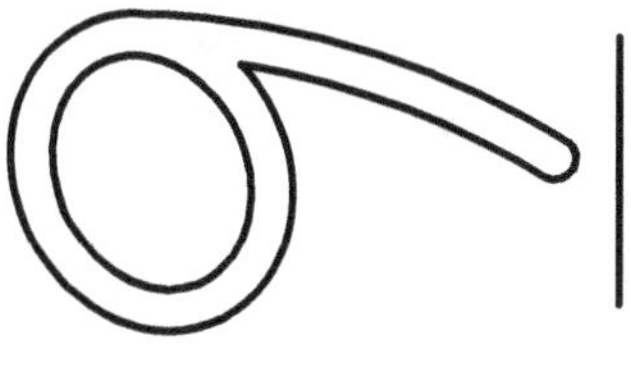

Alphabet Bingo
Letters N-R

q	o	n
r	r	p
n	P	o
R	N	Q
P	O	R
O	P	N

Alphabet Die

Letters N-R

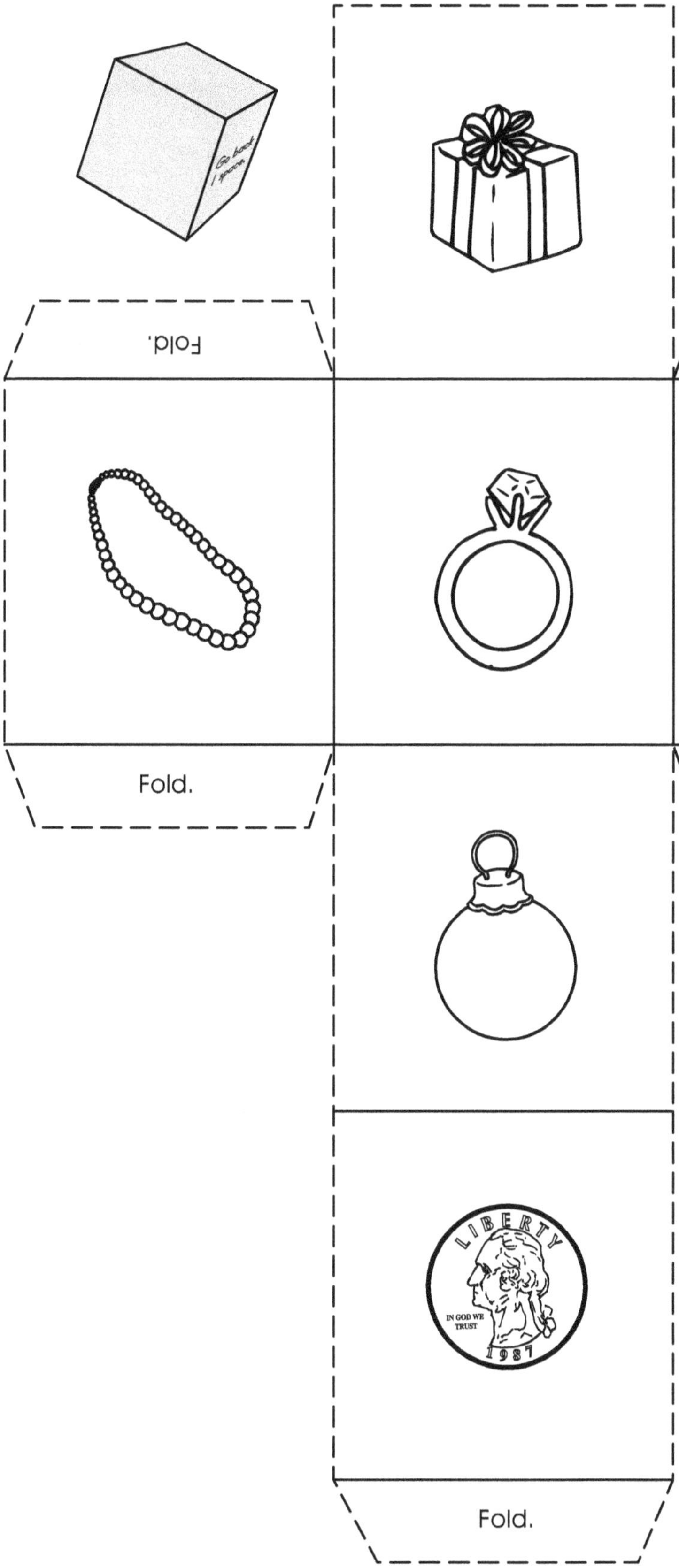

Go back
1 space.
Fold.
Fold.
Fold.
Fold.
Fold.
LIBERTY
IN GOD WE TRUST
1987

Glue or staple tops together.

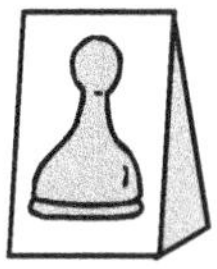

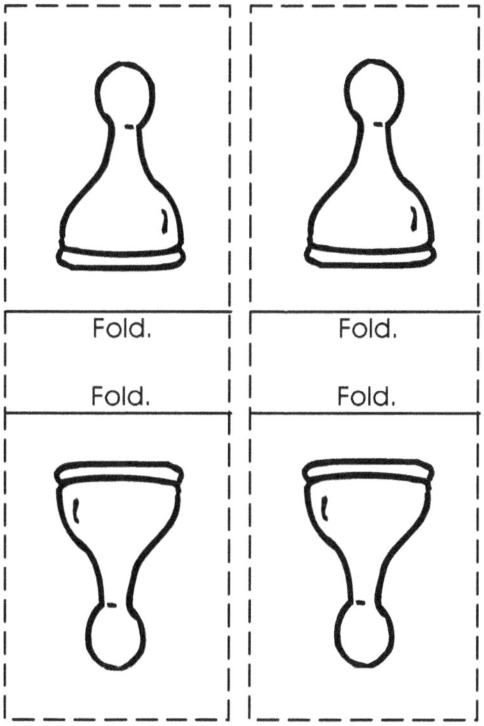

Fold.
Fold.
Fold.
Fold.

Color each pawn a different color.

Color-By-Letter
Letters N and O

Color the **N** shapes yellow. Color all the other shapes blue.

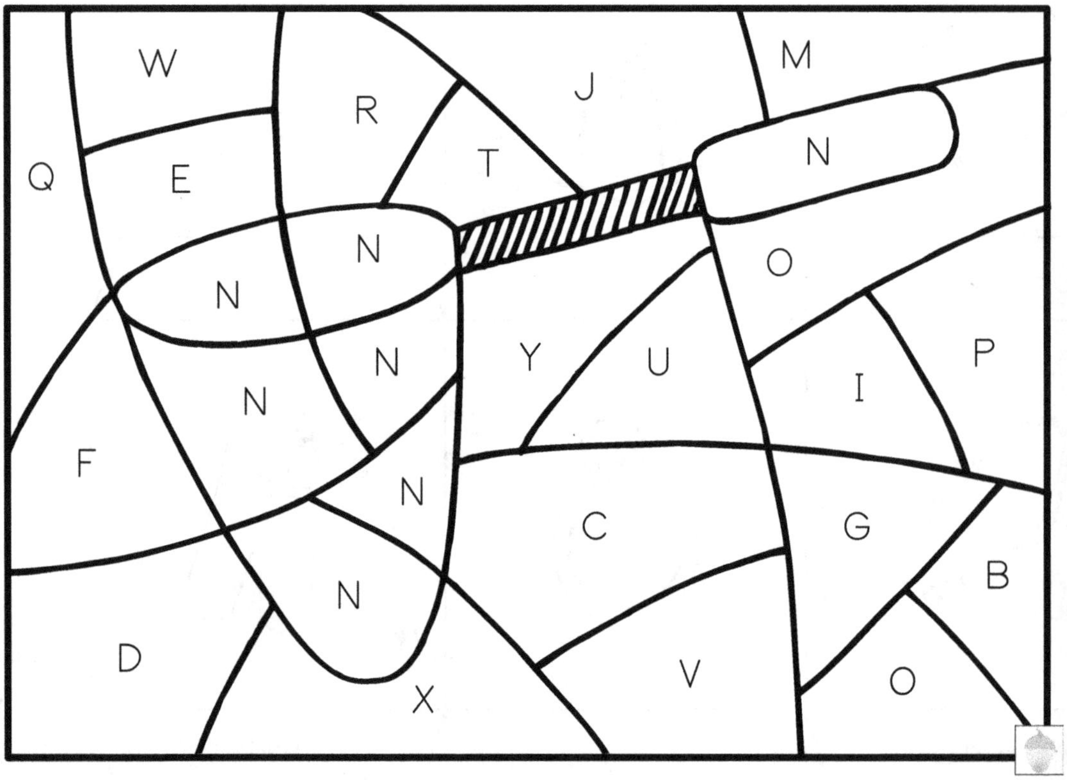

Color the **O** shapes orange. Color all the other shapes brown.

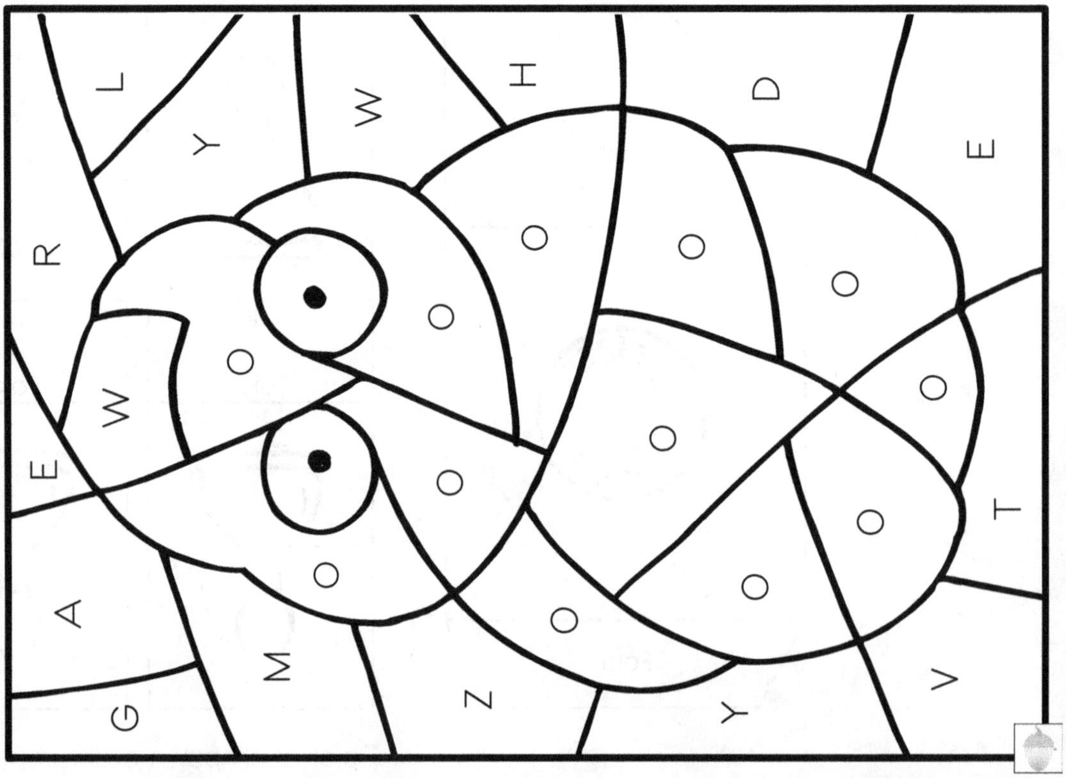

Color-By-Letter
Letters P-Q

Color the **P** shapes pink. Color all the other shapes brown.

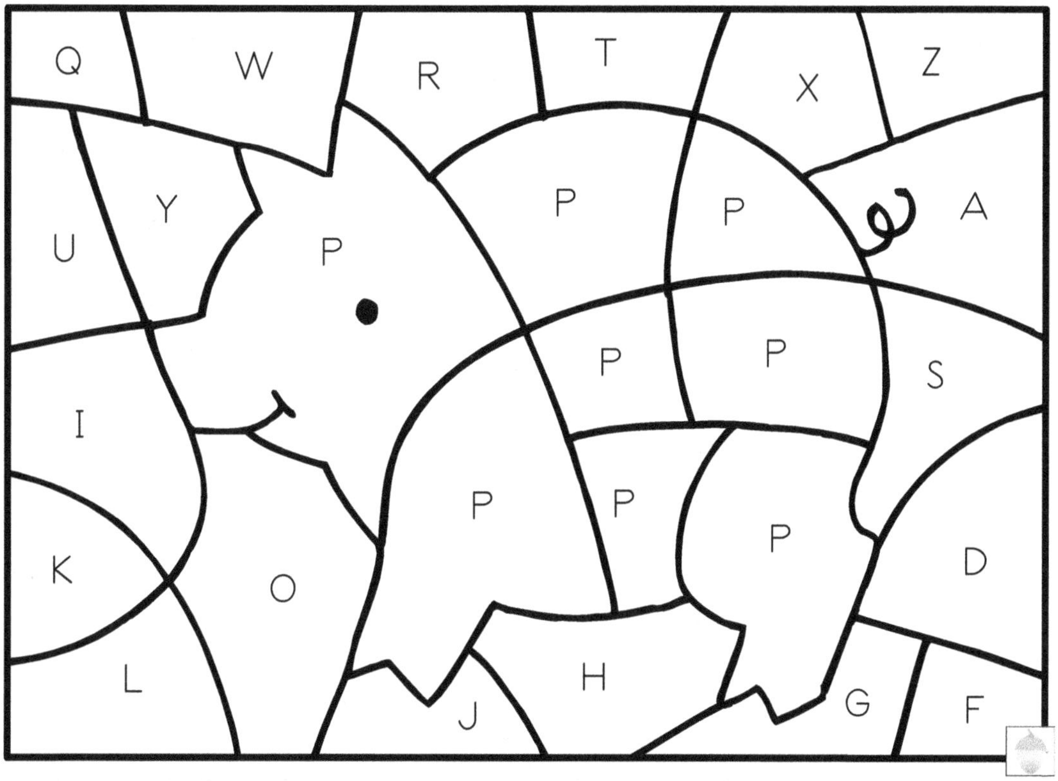

Color the **Q** shapes brown. Color all the other shapes yellow.

Color-By-Letter
Letter N-R

Color the **R** shapes white. Color all the other shapes pink.

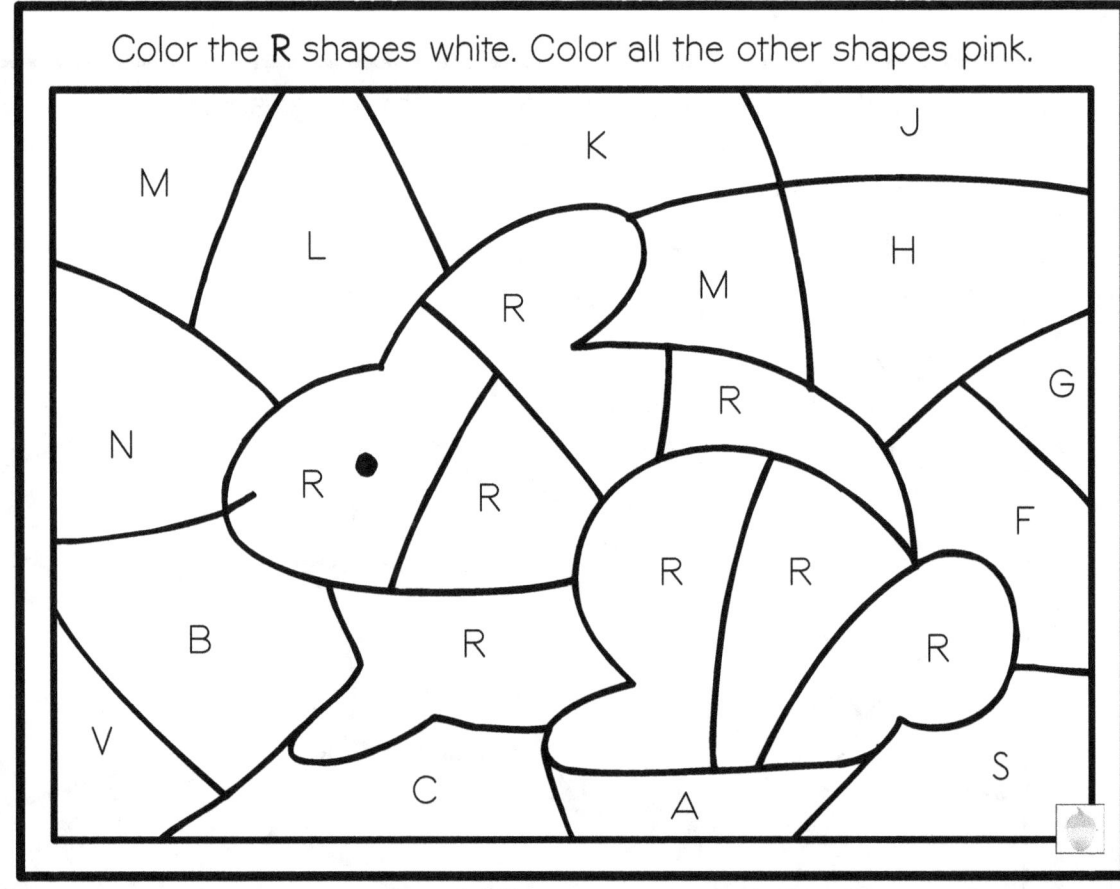

Color the **N** shape red.
Color the **O** shape orange.
Color the **P** shape yellow.

Color the **Q** shape green.
Color the **R** shapes blue.

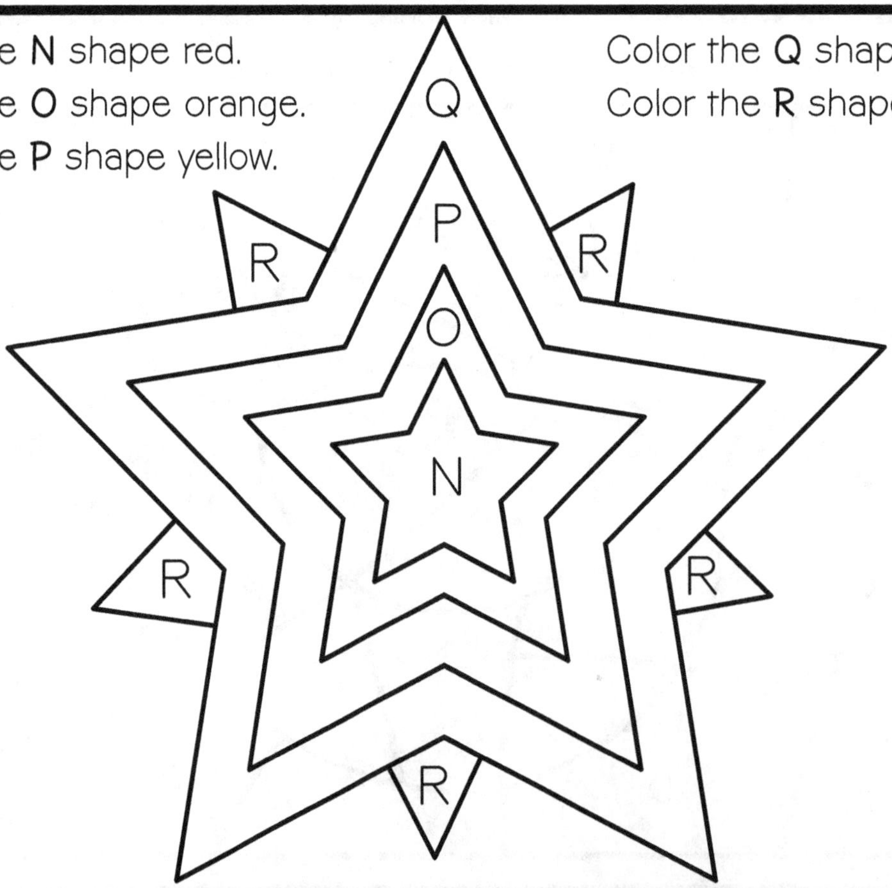

Alphabet Trail Game Board
Letters S-V

Follow the Alphabet Trail from S to V

START ↑

THE END

Alphabet Trail Game Board
Letters S-V

Place card deck, die, or spinner here.

Alphabet Trail Game Board

48   LAB20143P • ABC GAMES • 978-1-937257-59-0 • © 2014 Little Acorn Books™

Spinner and Pawns
Letters S-V

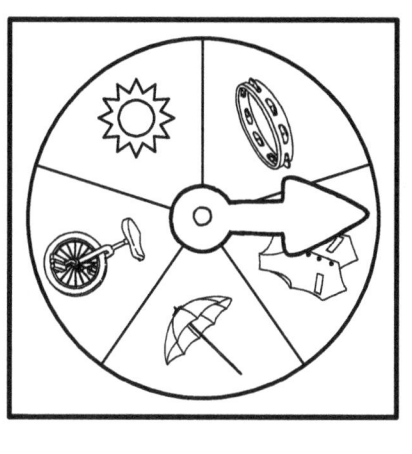
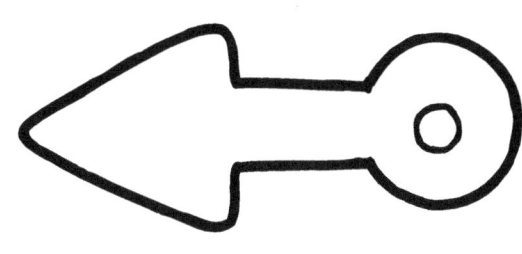
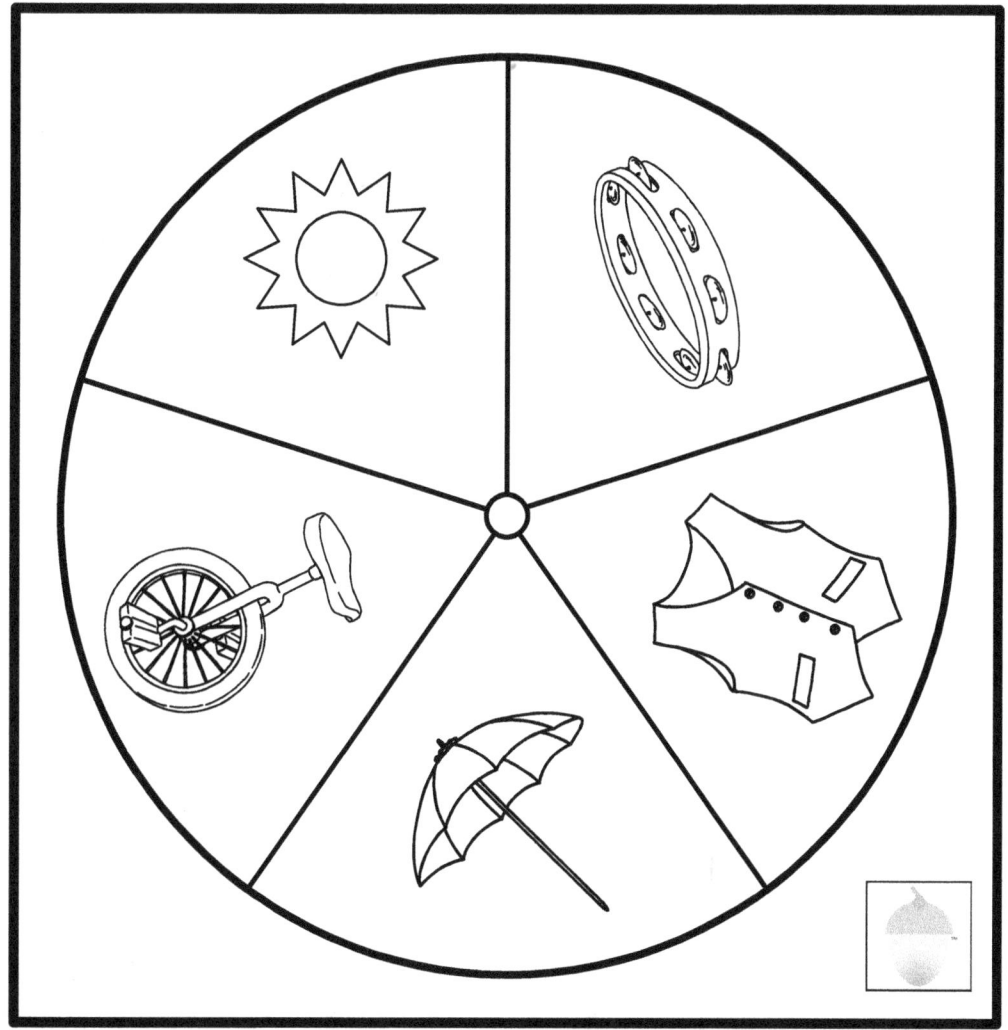

Color each pawn a different color.

Game Board Playing Cards
Letters S-V

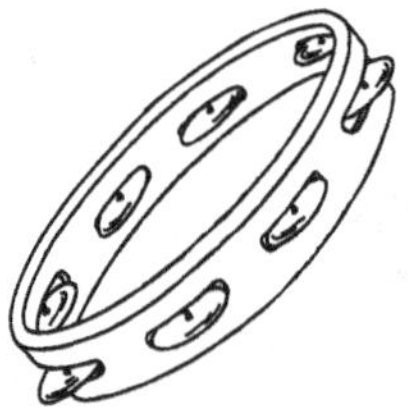

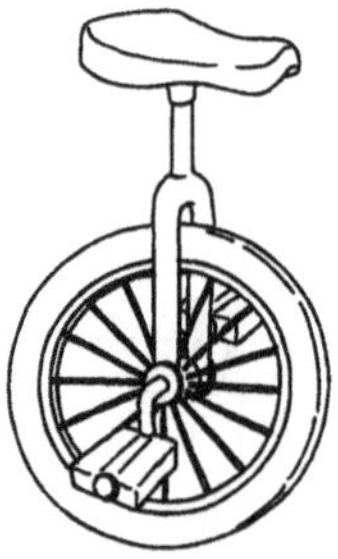

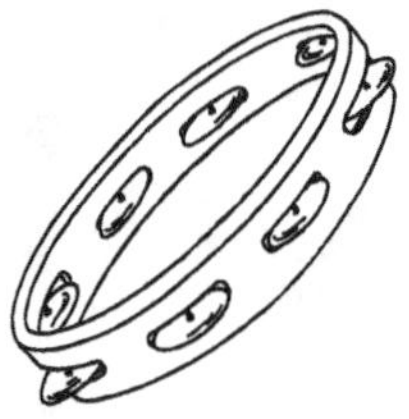

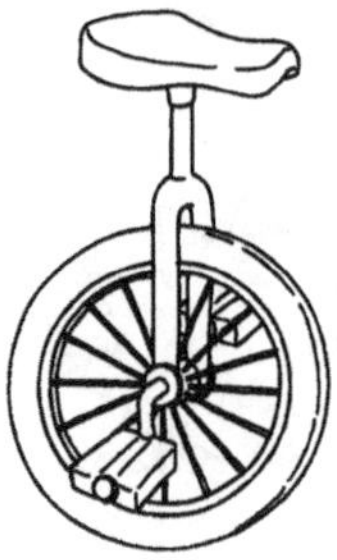

s t u v | Move forward 1 space.

S T U V | Move back 1 space.

50   LAB20143P • ABC GAMES • 978-1-937257-59-0 • © 2014 Little Acorn Books™

Alphabet Bingo

Alphabet Pictures S-V

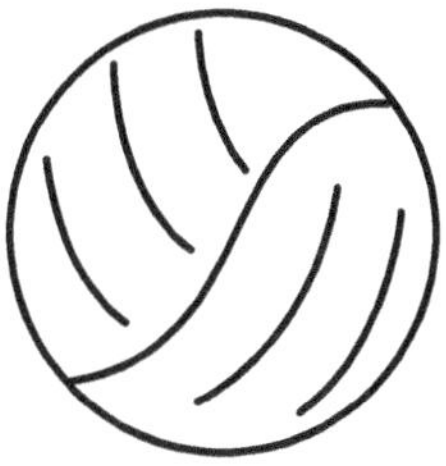

volleyball

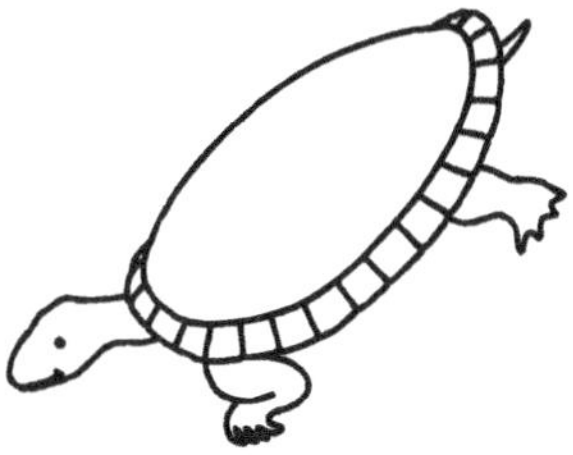

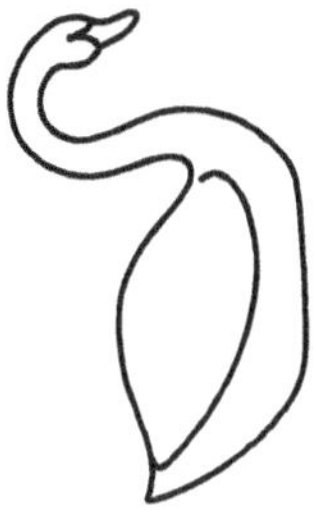

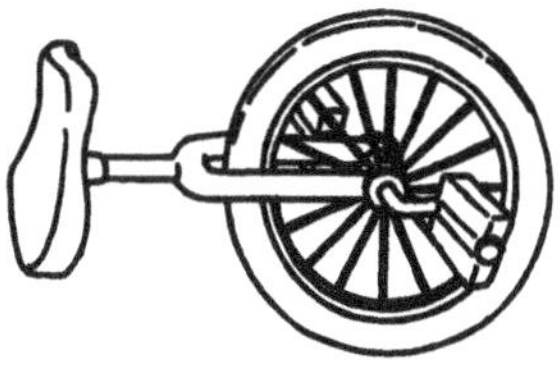

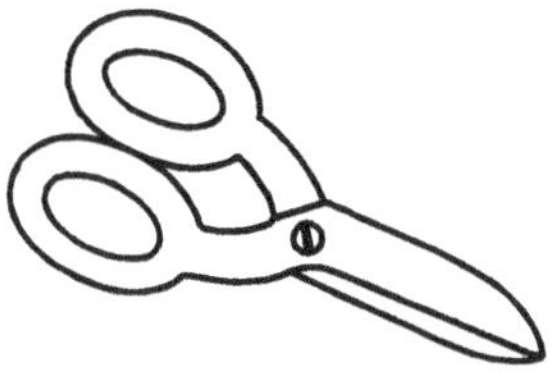

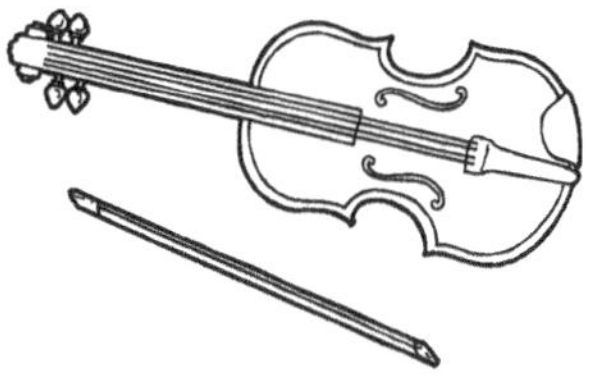

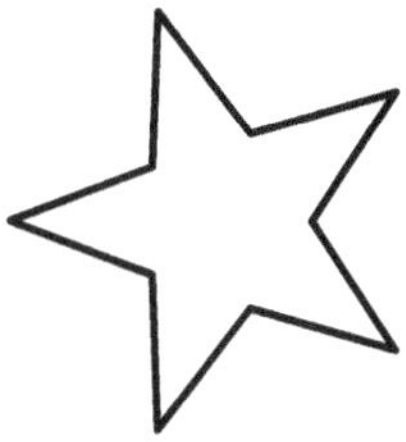

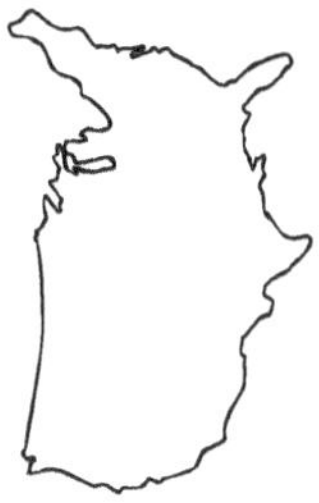

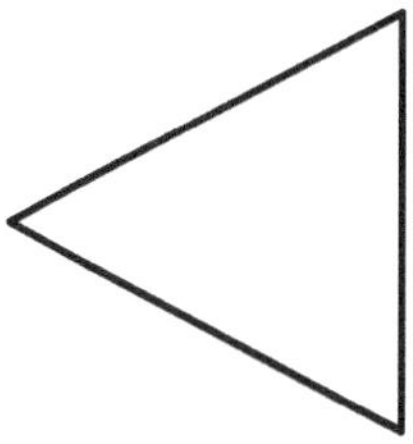

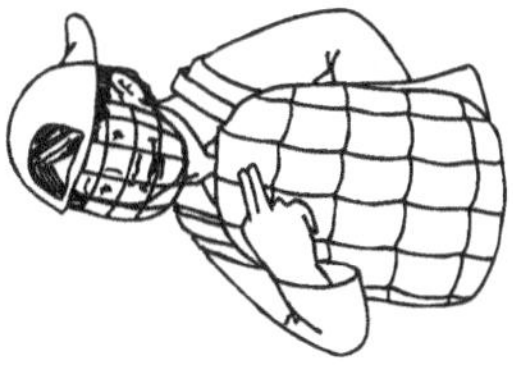

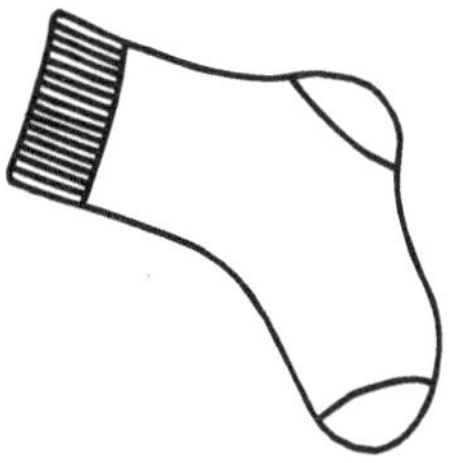

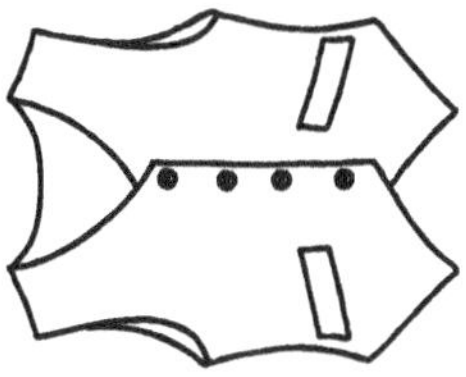

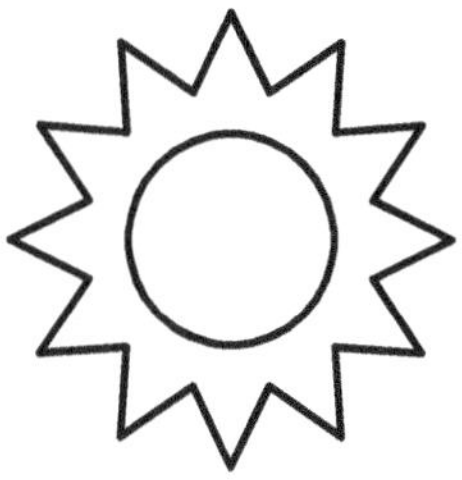

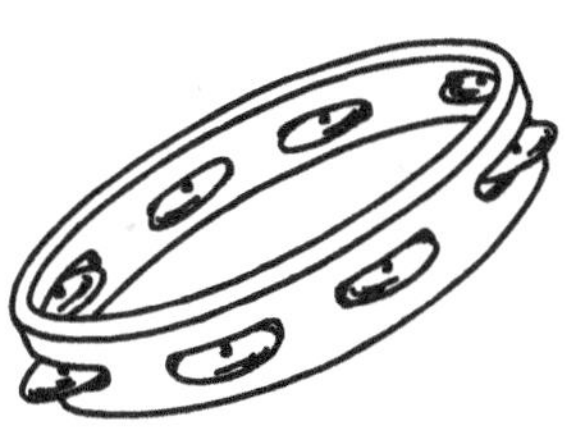

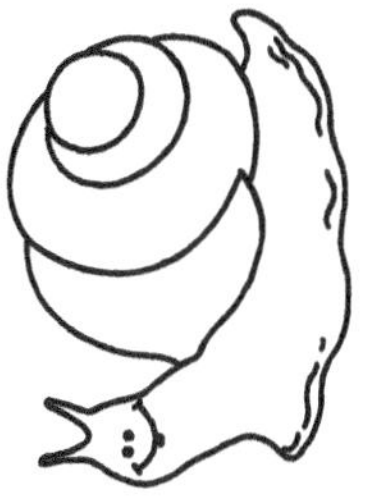

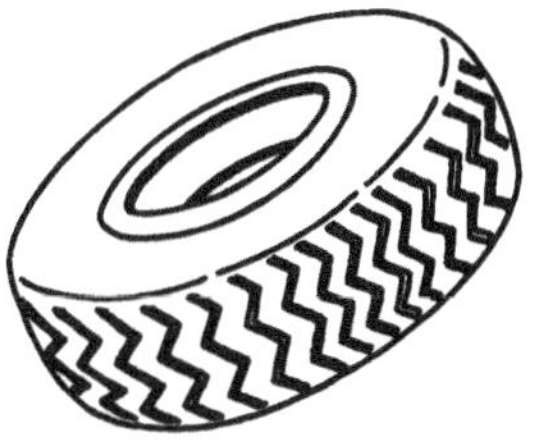

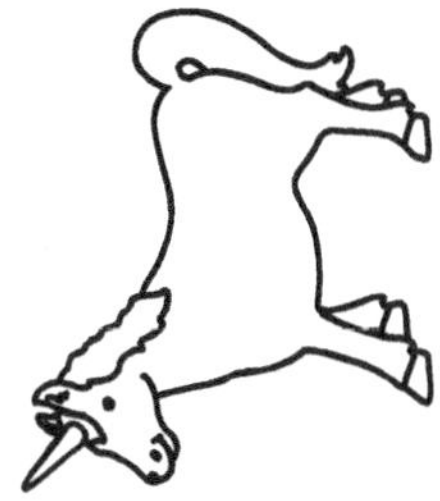

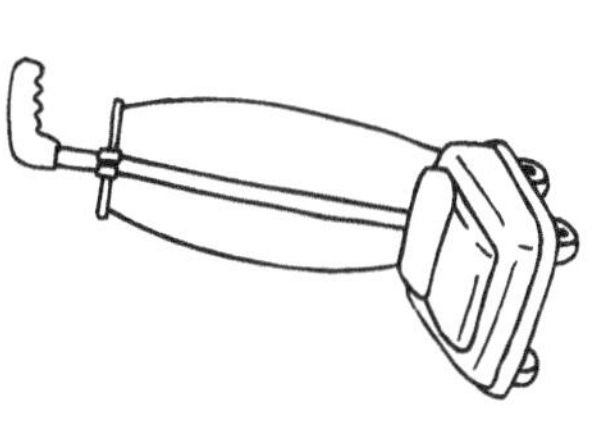

Alphabet Bingo
Letters S-V

v	t	s
u	s	v
s	u	t

U	S	V
S	T	S
T	U	V

52   LAB20143P • ABC GAMES • 978-1-937257-59-0 • © 2014 Little Acorn Books™

Alphabet Die
Letters S-V

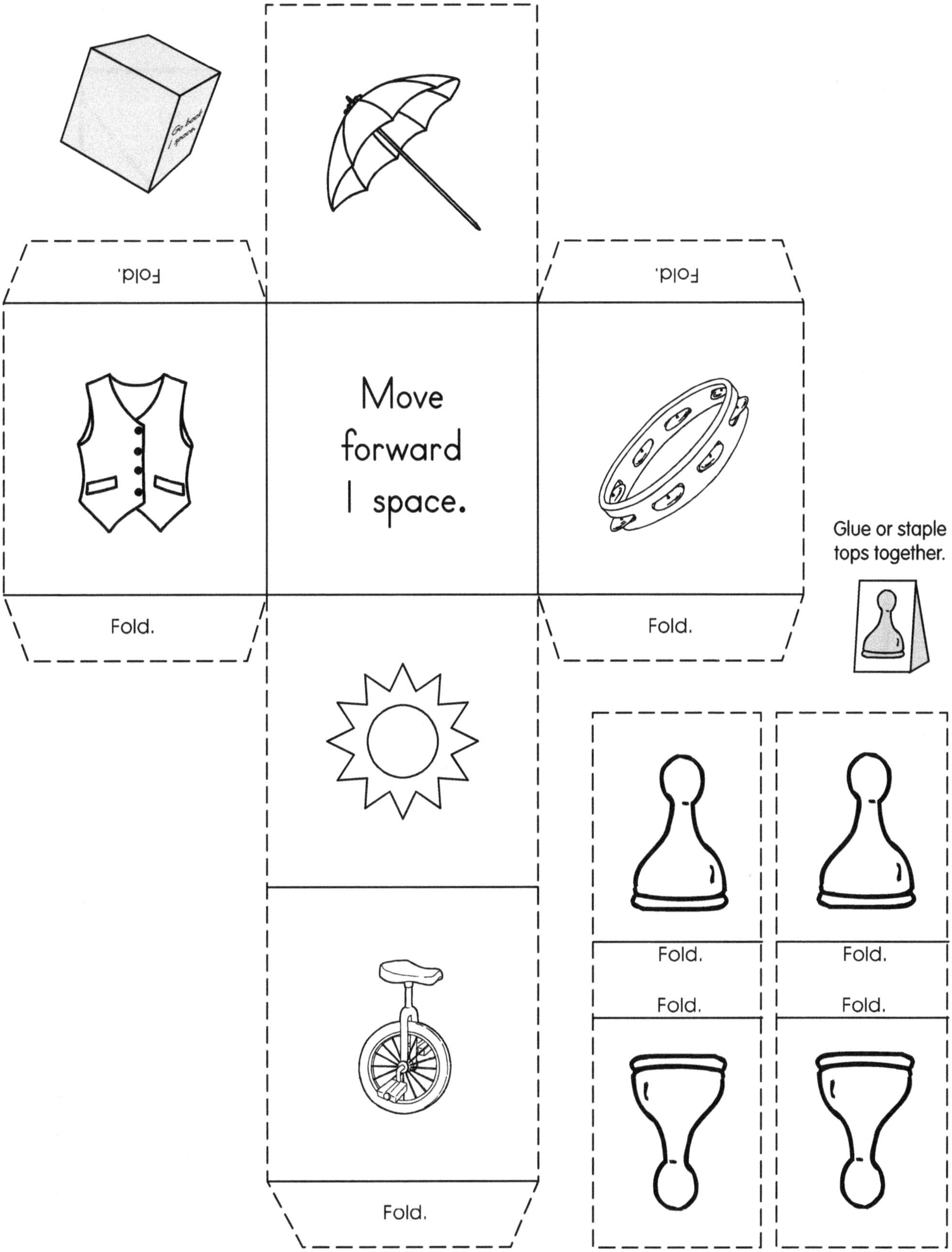

Move forward 1 space.

Fold.
Fold.
Fold.
Fold.
Fold.
Fold.
Fold.
Fold.
Fold.

Glue or staple tops together.

Color each pawn a different color.

Color-By-Letter
Letters S and T

Color the **S** shapes yellow. Color all the other shapes black.

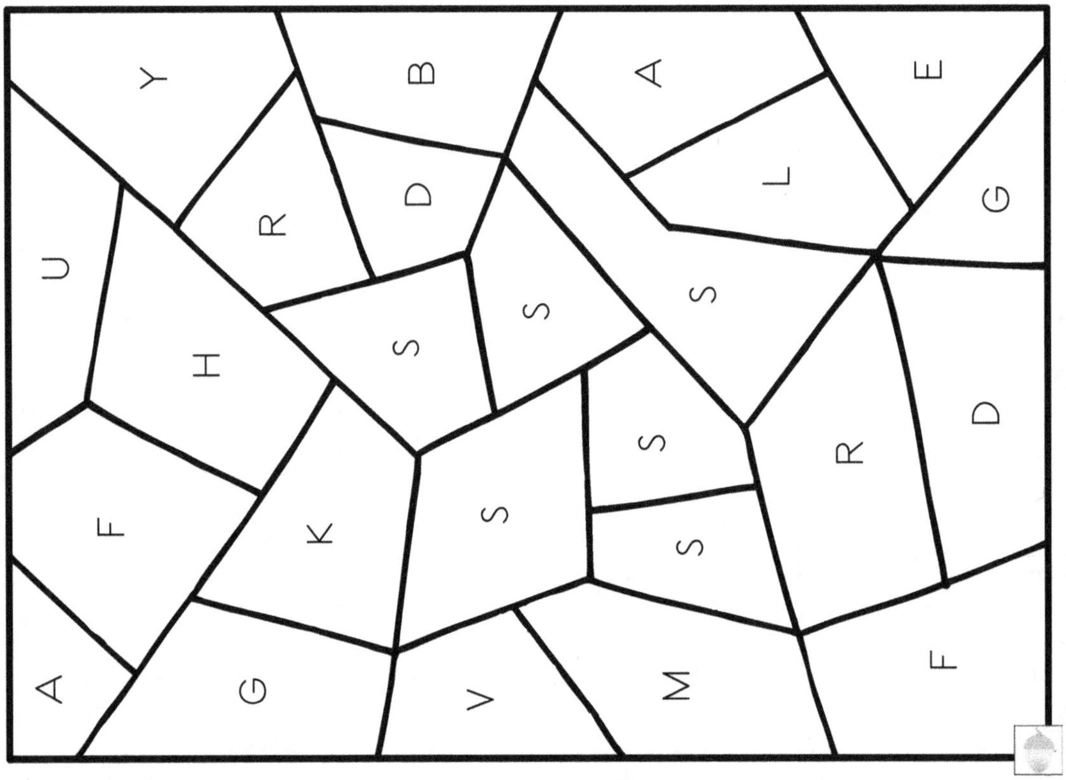

Color the **T** shapes green. Color all the other shapes blue.

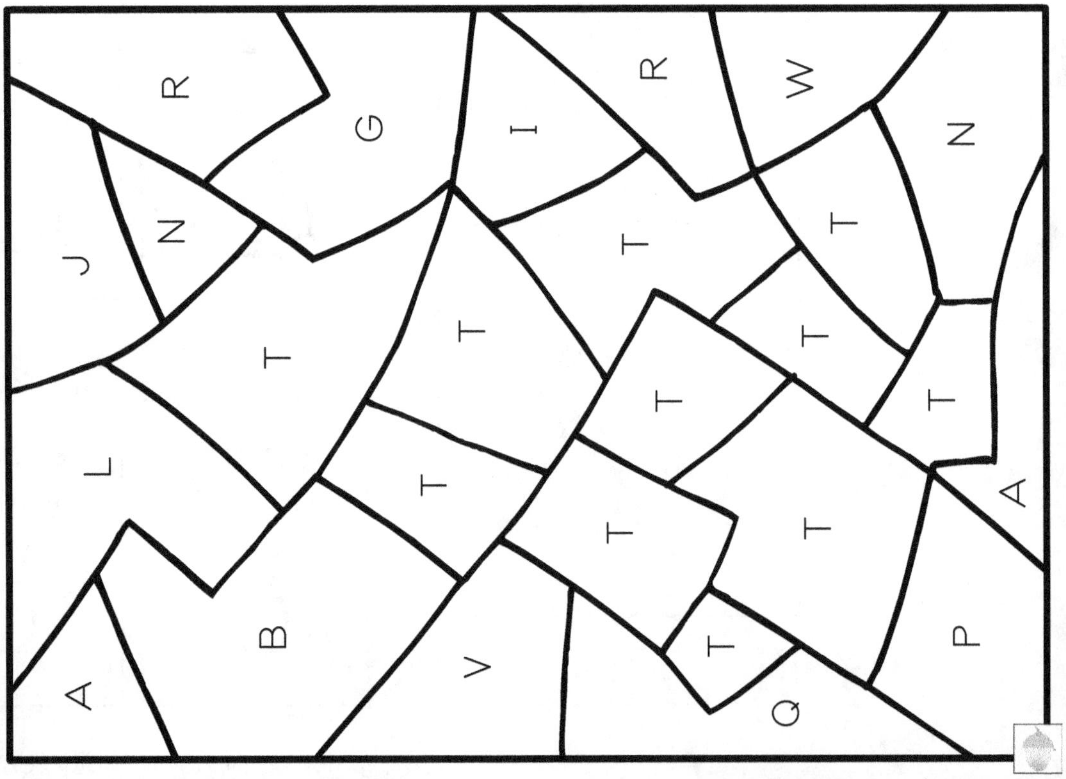

Color-By-Letter
Letters U and V

Color the **U** shapes purple. Color all the other shapes blue.

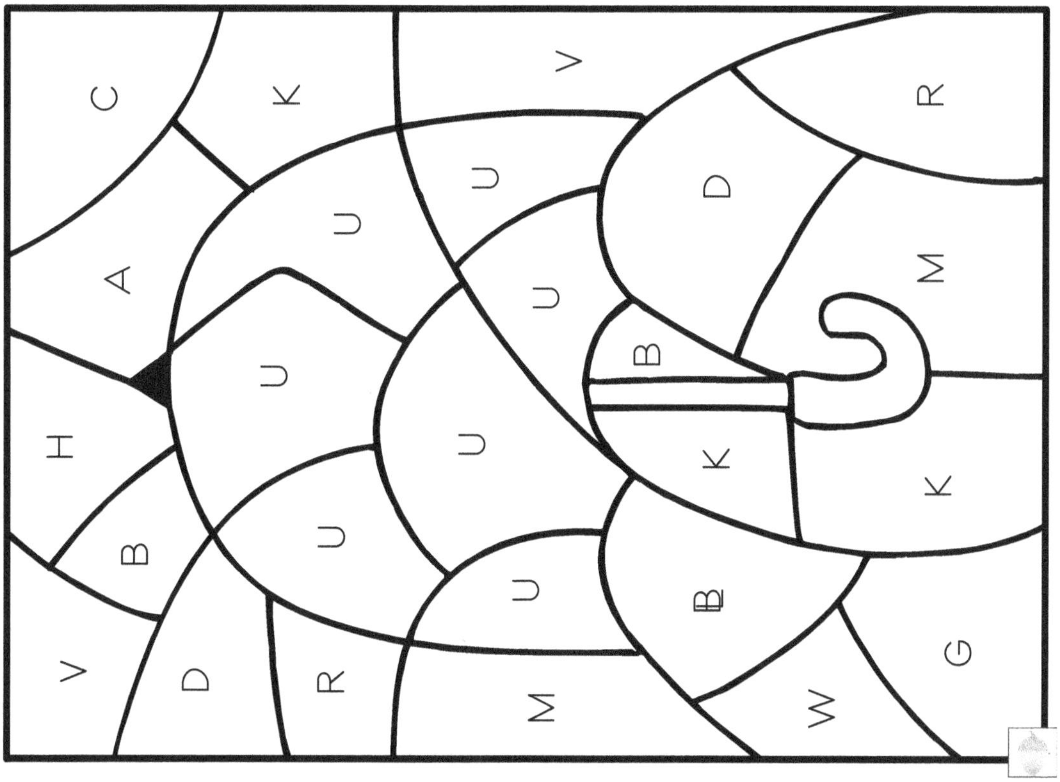

Color the **V** shapes green. Color all the other shapes red.

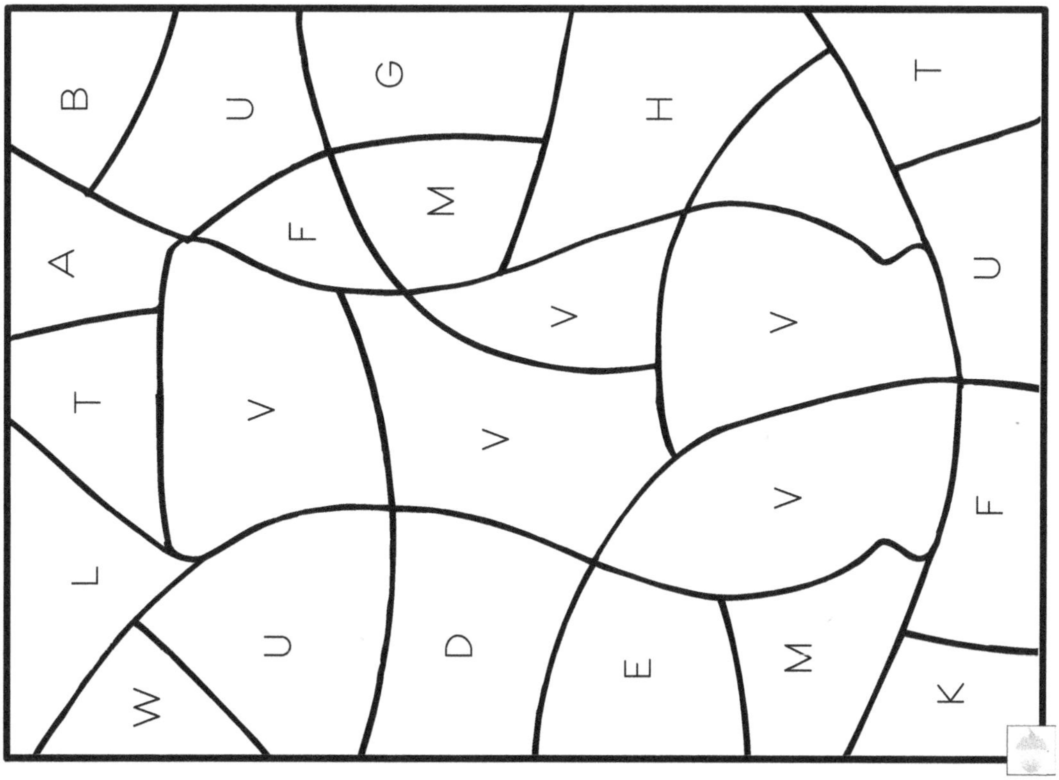

Color-By-Letter
Letters S-V

Color the **S** shapes red. Color the **T** shapes yellow. Color the **U** shapes orange. Color the **V** shapes green.

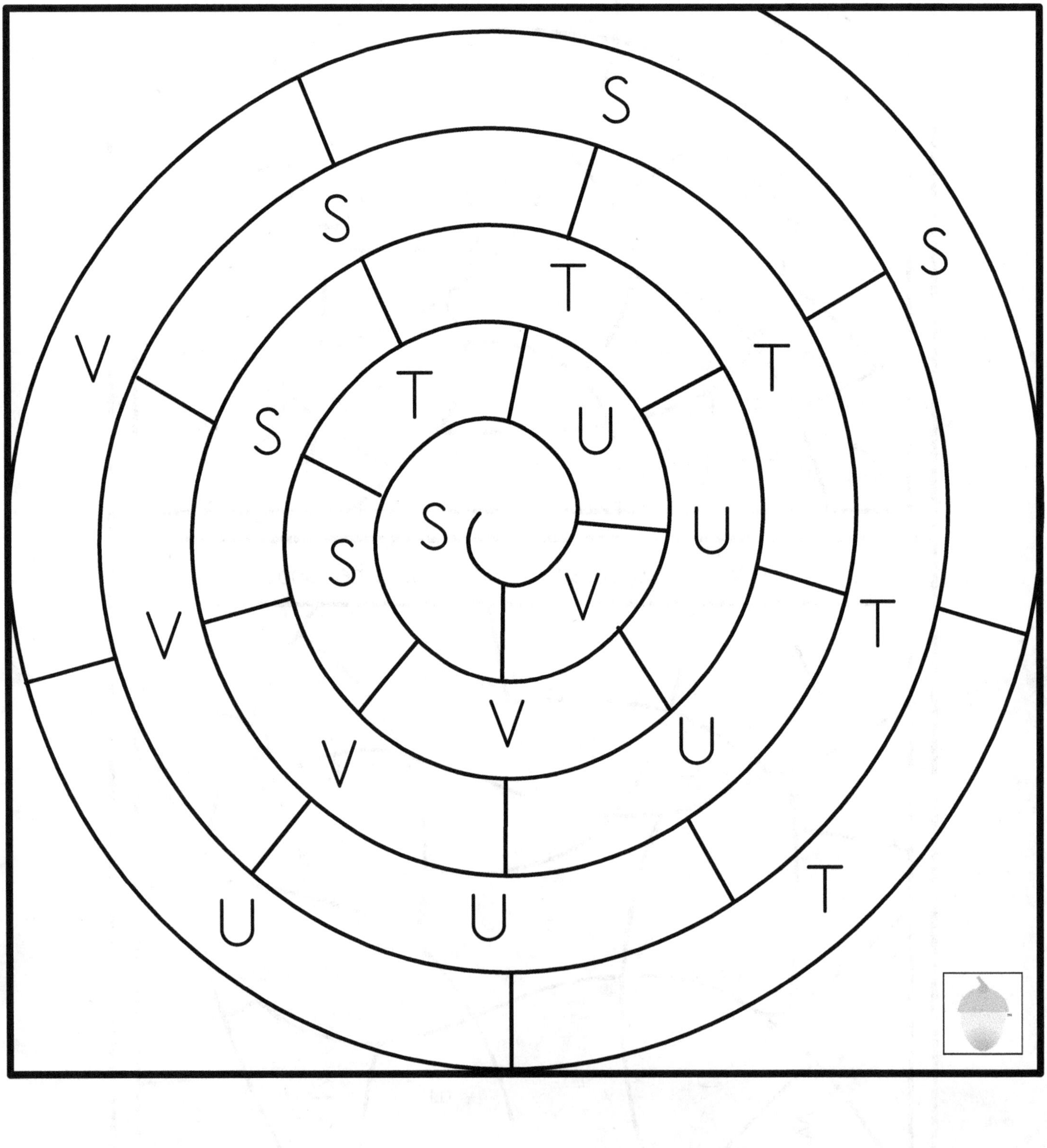

Alphabet Trail Game Board
Letters W-Z

Follow the Alphabet Trail from W to Z

START ↑ | THE END

Alphabet Trail Game Board
Letters W-Z

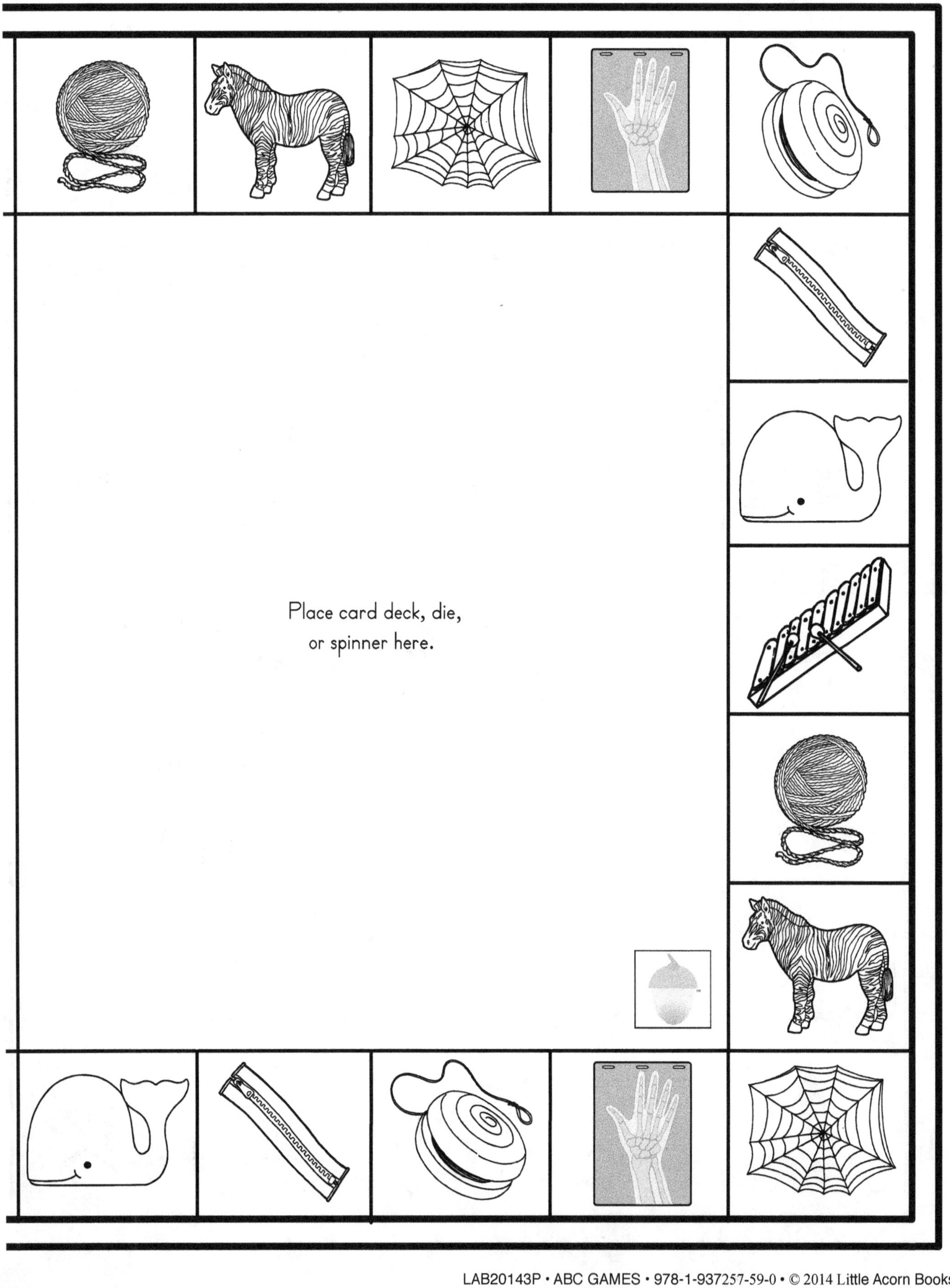

Place card deck, die, or spinner here.

Spinner and Pawns
Letters W-Z

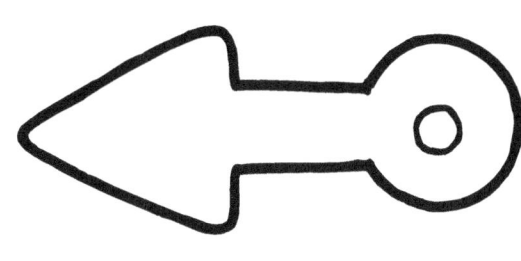
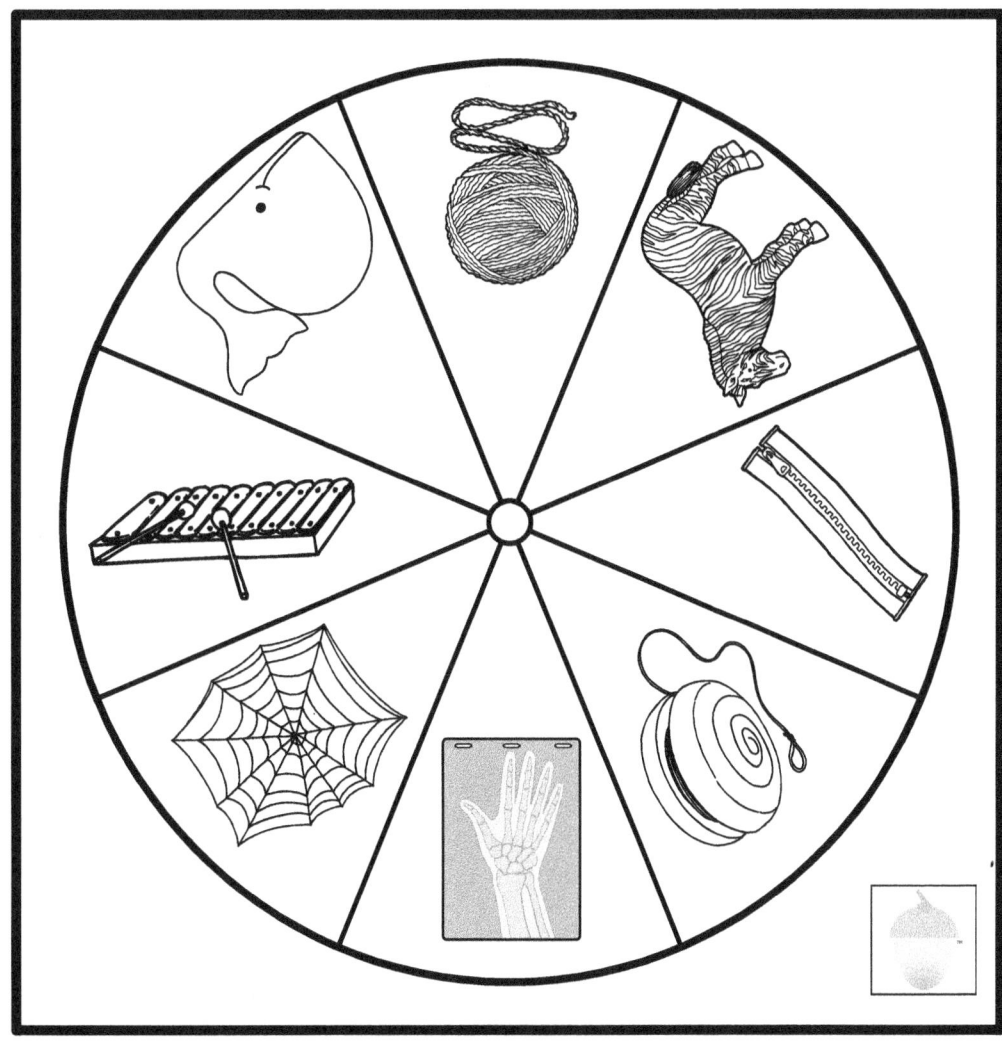

xantusia

yak

zebu

Color each pawn a different color.

Game Board Playing Cards
Letters W-Z

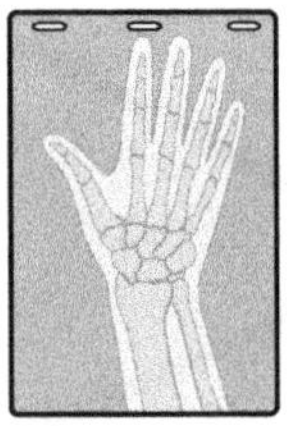

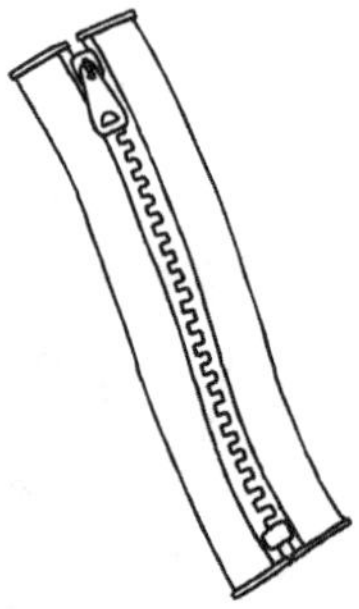

				Move forward 1 space.
				Move back 1 space.
w	x	y	z	Move forward 1 space.
W	X	Y	Z	Move back 1 space.

Alphabet Bingo
Alphabet Pictures W–Z

yak

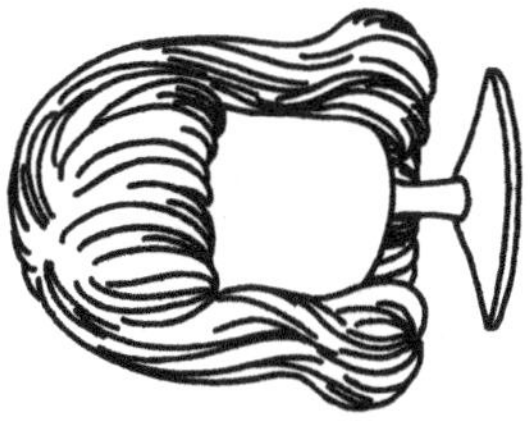

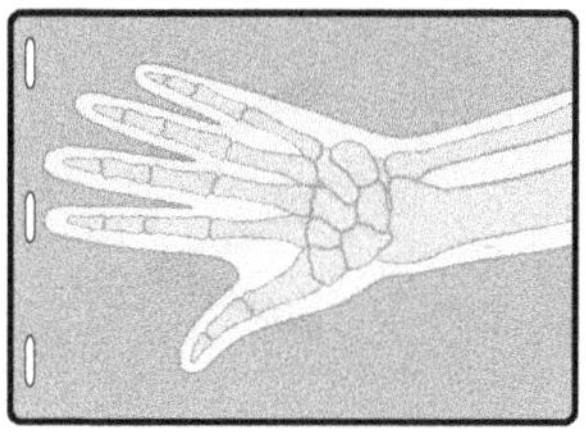

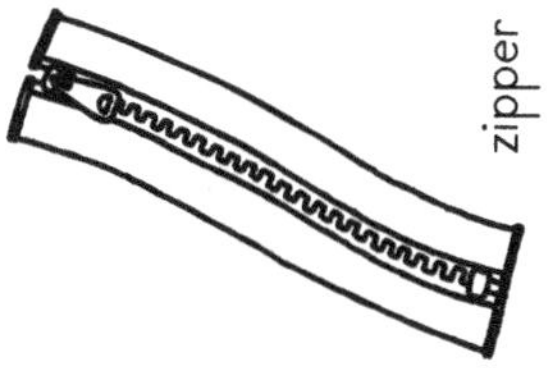

zipper

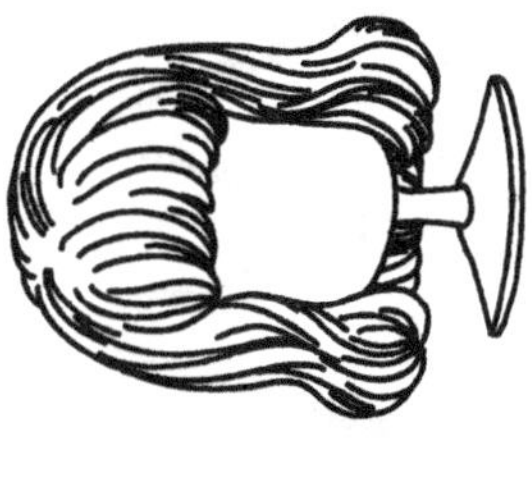

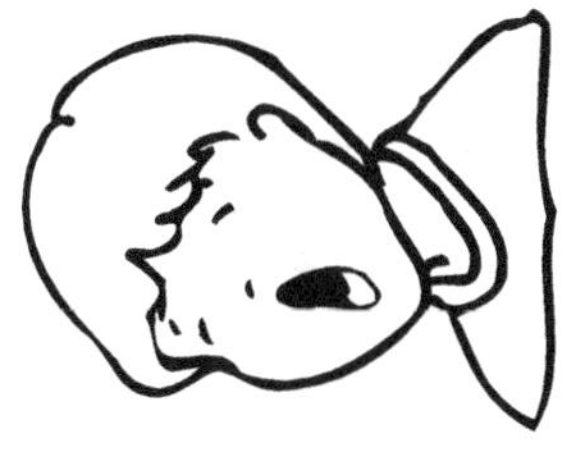

Alphabet Bingo
Letters W-Z

N	X	W
Y	W	W
W	Y	X
Y	W	N
W	W	W
X	Y	Y

Alphabet Die

Letters W-Z

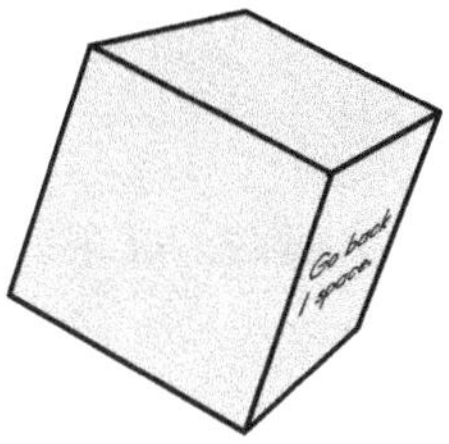

W

Fold.

Move forward 1 space.

X

Fold.

Go back 1 space.

Fold.

Fold.

Glue or staple tops together.

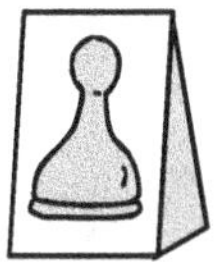

Y

Z

Fold.

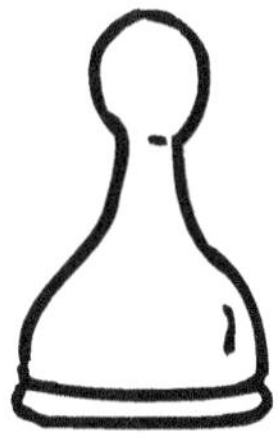

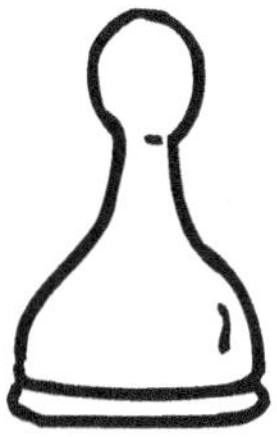

Fold.

Fold.

Fold.

Fold.

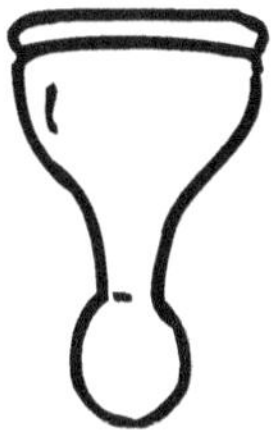

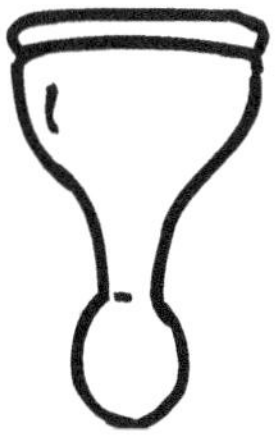

Color each pawn a different color.

Color-By-Letter
Letters W-Z

Color the **W** spaces pink. Color the **X** spaces blue.
Color the **Y** spaces yellow. Color the **Z** spaces purple.

Y	X	Y		Y	X		X
W			W			W	
Y	X	Y		Y	X		X
Z	Y	X	Z	X	Y	Z	Y
W			W			W	
Z	Y	X	Z	X	Y	Z	Y
Y	X	Y		Y	X		X
W			W			W	

Little Acorn Books™

Promoting Early Skills for a Lifetime™

A Hands-on Picture Book Series Designed to Foster Early Skills • Infancy–Age 4

Using Crayons, Scissors, & Glue for Crafts
Preschool–Grade 1

Miss Pitty Pat & Friends
Preschool–Grade 1

Mookie's Christmas Tree
Not Just for Christmas

Hands-On ABCs • ABC and Readiness Skills Practice for Early Learners

LAB20143P • ABC GAMES • 978-1-937257-59-0 • © 2014 Little Acorn Books™

www.ingramcontent.com/pod-product-compliance
Lightning Source LLC
Chambersburg PA
CBHW081455060426
42444CB00037BA/3287